Teaching
TENNIS
Protocol for Instructors

Steven White

equilibrium
books
A Division of Wish Publishing

Wish Publishing
Terre Haute, Indiana
www.wishpublishing.com

Library of Congress Control Number: 2008931618

Edited by Heather Lowhorn

Editorial assistance provided by Dorothy Chambers

Cover designed by Phil Velikan

Printed in the United States of America
10 9 8 7 6 5 4 3 2 1

Published in the United States by
Equilibrium Books, A Division of Wish Publishing
P.O. Box 10337
Terre Haute, IN 47801, USA
www.wishpublishing.com

Distributed in the United States by
Cardinal Publishers Group
2402 N. Shadeland Avenue
Indianapolis, Indiana 46219
www.cardinalpub.com

Table of Contents

Introduction

The ability to play tennis at a high performance level is an acquired skill that takes years of experience to master. Acquiring the ability to teach the game with a high degree of skill can be just as difficult. In fact, helping other players to develop their skills can be more difficult than developing your own. Just because you were a better-than-average player doesn't mean that you have what it takes to promote the skills of others. *Teaching Tennis: Protocol for Instructors* is the product of over 25 years of tennis teaching experience. Steven White, a certified instructor with the Professional Tennis Registry, has created a guide for coaches and established instructors who want to improve the efficiency and effectiveness of their teaching abilities, and for players who want to become teachers.

Steven strives toward excellence in sharing his system of teaching tennis. Because he is serious about helping his students learn the game of tennis in a clear and understandable way, he explains the game with a no-nonsense attitude and high professional standards. This guide covers six different areas that are essential to anyone seeking to become a better instructor or coach.

PART 1 — TEACHING A CLASS OR GROUP

This part discusses many areas of tennis camp and clinic protocol, including respecting your clients, giving lessons, demonstrating and explaining techniques, court safety, using equipment, making corrections, speaking to groups, and organization. All commentary is directed toward potential staff to give the reader a better mental view of how a camp should be run.

PART 2 — ESSENTIALS OF THE GAME

This section covers grips, stances, footwork and movement, ground strokes, playing at net, the serve and service return. With incisive commentary and photo illustrations, each stroke is broken down in understandable terms.

PART 3 — WORKING WITH JUNIORS

This section covers information associated with the phases of player development, practice techniques, game styles and performance. All of these elements begin to reveal themselves as a player enters the teen years, and every instructor should be equipped with the knowledge to take that player to the next level of competition.

PART 4 — CONDITIONING, FITNESS AND STRENGTH TRAINING

PART 5 — NUTRITION

PART 6 — COMMON TENNIS INJURIES

Recognizing that some coaches come to the courts without a complete knowledge of general sports science issues, these three sections covers conditioning, fitness, strength training, nutrition, hydration, and prevention and treatment of common tennis injuries.

The information found in this book will help you become a stronger teacher, which in turn will help your students reach their full potential.

Part 1
Teaching a Class or Group

Always remember that as instructors and coaches, we are privileged to work for our students. Young people come to us for instruction during an important time in their lives. That alone demands special treatment. Remember that they are your clients and treat them with respect. Avoid condescending tones and comments and speak in normal terms rather than using confused, unintelligible language. Strive to develop a special tennis relationship with each student. If you have more than one student in a class, be sure to give all the students the same amount of attention — even though some may need more than others. Try not to play favorites, and care about the improvement of each and every student.

As an instructor, you must be able to execute and explain all the strokes. Whenever you can, practice your own shot-making and work to improve your abilities. The students need to see what properly executed strokes should look like. Using good form yourself is essential in teaching others.

Appearance is important. Try to look as professional as possible. Wear only proper tennis attire on the courts to promote neatness to your students.

If you are not a professional instructor, make every effort to be informed about fields that are related to tennis. Be aware of new developments in stroke production, teaching techniques and sports science. Read tennis publications and keep up with the current events of the sport. This will help you continue to improve and it always makes for good conversation with your students.

GIVING LESSONS

Organization is the key to giving an effective lesson. Give the students appropriate information and clear instructions. Keep it simple and make presentations that are in proper sequence. Do not confuse the class with too much information. Help each student as much as you can. Make sure they understand the point you are trying to make and feel they are achieving their goals.

When giving your lessons, be observant. Watch the students during their shot-making so that you can give them proper advice. When a student has a question, give him or her the answer immediately. Students are receiving a lot of information, and you may have to explain the same thing over and over again. Give your students as many shots as possible. Always use a high volume of balls, run your classes with a quick tempo, and always have a number of drills in mind.

Set the right tone for the lesson before the first ball is struck. If the proper tone is set at the beginning of the lesson, you will have a better chance of maintaining it throughout. After the introductions, tell the students what the class will cover and start an activity. If one or more of the students is running a little late, rather than holding up the group, you can occupy their time with some questions and answers or by reviewing the previous lesson. The best thing to do is to get them on the court for a few minutes of warm-up. In any case, the idea is to get their attention early and keep it.

At the beginning of the lesson, it is generally a good idea to avoid long-winded explanations and discussions. Get the students moving or playing as soon as possible. Some of your students might be a little nervous. Notice how quickly they relax after they begin to hit some balls. If your group members are novice players, mass drill formations are useful to practice swings, footwork and techniques.

Practice swings will give the students a chance to train their muscles in the proper motions and patterns. And since the drill is not fast-paced, it offers students the opportunity to ask questions. If there's more than one instructor on the court during the mass drill, each should circulate and speak with the students individually to note specific corrections. As the lesson progresses, the instructor should focus on maintaining the tempo. End the lesson on a positive and exciting note. The instructor should always allocate a little time for discussion and review of the new material covered. Be sure to answer every student's questions. Don't leave anyone hanging.

If you are working with other instructors, communicate with them! Each instructor should know — and agree upon — the basics of shot-making: grips, stroke production, swing patterns, footwork, movement and strategies. I can't stress enough the importance of all the instructors giving the same accurate information.

DEMONSTRATING AND EXPLAINING TECHNIQUES

No matter what the stroke, proper demonstration is essential. Demonstrations are excellent introductions to new material and to the instructional points to be covered in the lesson. A good demonstration sets a clear image for the student and provides a good example of what they should be trying to do. Demonstrate strokes by dropping and hitting the ball yourself or by having another instructor hit balls to you. Help the students watch the demonstration by directing their attention to different points. Tell them to watch your feet, racquet, wrist or swing pattern. Help them to identify the important parts of the stroke and explain how the stroke is different from or similar to what they already know. Demonstrations can include members of the group. If one of the students has good technique, let him or her show the others. Doing this will give the others the feeling that they can develop good technique as well.

It is important that your explanations be direct and simple. Focus on specific details, but give the students an overall description of the material. Tell the students how the drill will work and where they should position themselves from the beginning to the end of each drill.

No matter how clear your instructions, following directions can be difficult. Be patient and ready to repeat your instructions. Some drills are complicated, especially for novices. In addition to explaining what will happen, you may still have to work through the pattern with everyone. When you're working with groups of students, rotating through the drill can be confusing for them. Be sure that each student knows how to follow the rotation.

Good questions can encourage everyone's understanding and help develop student-instructor relations, but unnecessary and prolonged questions can break the flow of the lesson. Do not spend too much time on any one question. Give everyone a chance to ask as many questions as they need, but if a question does not apply to the current class, try to tactfully and politely put it off until later. Regardless of how basic the question is, never be sarcastic or flippant in your answer. Answer all questions directly and politely. Do not be condescending or leave the student with the impression that you look down on their lack of understanding.

SAFETY ON THE COURT

Other than muscle strains and heat-related illnesses, most injuries that occur on the tennis court are ball-related. When a large number of balls are being used, particular attention should be given to the positioning of the students, especially if it is the students' first visit to the court or their first time doing the drill. At the beginning of each drill, be sure to remind everyone of the hazards involved. Tell the students to help keep the court as clean as possible without disrupting the flow of the drill. Ask them to help clear the balls off the court whenever possible. Caution them about the balls at their feet and tell them to warn others who might have balls near their feet. Some drills require that the students be close to the net or close to each other. When it is their turn to hit the ball, remind them to be aware of the other students and to exit the court in the opposite direction of the oncoming ball. Ask the students to move off to the side and away from the net to get out of the line of fire. When the students have been assigned to pick up balls, ask them to be aware of their position related to the drills going on around them.

While the lesson is in progress, it is important to keep an eye open for potentially dangerous situations that might develop. Warn the students about special hazards on or around the courts, such as benches, trash cans, fences, ball hoppers, ball carts and ball machines. Ball machines can be particularly hazardous when operated improperly. Inform the students of the ball machine's possible dangers and show them how to properly load the machines. On windy days, keep an eye open for blown balls that are rolling onto the court while the drill is in progress. When dealing with kids, remind them never to horseplay or hit balls at others. This is a common experience at all tennis camps. All kids should be warned that there will be time-out consequences for this behavior. When positioning your students, be sure they are not so close to each other that someone could get hit by a swinging racquet.

During the extreme hot summer months, make sure the students are aware of the dangers of overexposure to the sun. Dehydration, fatigue, muscle strains and blisters are all heat-related conditions that require first-aid materials. It is the instructor's responsibility to make sure containers of water are available to the students and positioned near the courts in a safe area. In all situations, it is the instructor's responsibility to maintain a group consciousness regarding safety.

USING EQUIPMENT

Although there will never be a replacement for one-on-one instruction from a certified teaching professional, ball machines can be a great asset. Ball machines can be an instructor's best friend and a useful tool in developing a student's skills. When using a machine, be familiar with the abilities of the group with which you are working and set the machine accordingly. Placing ball machines in the proper location can ensure beneficial practice for the students. The type of drill will determine the position of the ball machine, and the instructor can choose the appropriate ball delivery frequency and speed for the students. Be sure that the machine is placed far enough away from the students to give them plenty of time to prepare for their shot-making. When starting a class, the machine should probably be set at lower speeds until the students become used to the flight of the ball, especially when the students are practicing volleys at the net. Even with the improvement of modern ball machines, the settings sometimes change themselves without adjustment by the instructor. Inform the students of this possibility and continually check the operation of the machine.

Don't allow a ball machine to let you become lazy. Just because a machine is in use doesn't mean it's break time for the instructors. In fact, all instructors should take advantage of the time to communicate with each student individually.

Placing ball hoppers and carts in the proper position is important for efficiency, convenience and safety. The positioning of the supply of balls is essential to keep the lesson flowing smoothly. The instructor should have a hopper or cart at his or her free arm's side, close enough so that reaching for balls is fast and efficient. Both the hopper and the instructor should be at the side of the court far from the student's line of fire. In serving drills, students often stand too close to the hoppers. Make sure each student is clear from the possibility of striking the hoppers or each other. In strategy drills, the hoppers should be conveniently placed far enough behind the baseline that no player is in danger of running into them.

INSTRUCTING

The ability to work with groups (as opposed to individuals) is a learned skill. Keeping the group moving and interested is an essential part of a successful lesson. Usually the drills are conducted at a moderate to fast pace, so efficiency is key. Equipment and people have to be in designated areas. Never stand in front of the students or in the way of their shots, except when demonstrating volleys. The students should not have to worry about hitting you or others. Whether you're feeding or hitting, stand far enough to the side that you will not be a target for the person with whom you are working or for those practicing with a ball machine. The instructor must be particularly careful positioning himself during overhead smash drills. When feeding balls, it is important to position yourself far enough away from the students that they will have plenty of time to prepare for their shot-making. Position your students with their backs to the sun, especially when the drills include serving or overhead smashes.

Feed the balls to your students according to the skill level of the class. When feeding to players of little or no skill, hit the ball to them softly. If the player has developed a moderate to advanced skill level, make adjustments to your ball feeding. Make sure that when feeding balls, the hopper is close enough to your side that you can easily reach them to keep from disrupting the flow of the drill. Feed rapidly enough to keep the students moving and to give them the opportunity to find some rhythm and build confidence. Try to make the drill challenging enough to facilitate improvement, but not so challenging that they become discouraged. Don't get caught up in instructing on stroke production alone. Integrate advice on footwork where it needs to be applied to improve their stroke production.

When hitting to the students, it is best to hit the ball off the bounce. This gives the students practice in viewing the ball as it leaves your racquet and helps them time their swings. All shots should be hit as accurately as possible and should be placed in exactly the right location for the student. Of course, never hit a ball toward a student without making sure that he or she is ready. Hit all shots at moderate pace and spin unless otherwise required. Be capable of hitting drives, topspins and backspins so that the students can practice all required plays on the ball.

Whenever possible try to rally with the students. They will be excited to play against the instructor and will probably try their hardest in that situation. Always control the pace and action on the ball so that the students get maximum practice. Play seriously whenever rallying with the students and set a good example for them to imitate.

After the students understand the mechanics of the strokes, they should be given the chance to put the strokes to use correctly and accurately. Of course, most people enjoy hitting out on the majority of their shots when they are practicing. Thus, they may be reluctant to reduce the pace of their shots to work on control. Yet the challenge of a target has such a universal appeal that most students will work hard to master the drill. Of course, the targets that are used must be kept to a reasonable level of difficulty for the students. Most enjoy a moderate percentage of success, so keep the targets large and close enough. In addition to giving the students experience in hitting shots to specific locations on the court, targets help the players focus on what action they must impart on the ball for placement. Assign a certain kind of shot to be hit; for example, a safe topspin drive crosscourt or a slice backhand down the lie. Change the target area after a few minutes to keep the students' interest sharp. Cones placed on the court are great targets for serving practice. Have the students keep up with the misses to determine a percentage rate of success. Hitting for accuracy or under pressure sometimes shows what the students will do when playing in matches. At times have them hit at full force to show the decrease in accuracy when overhitting.

CORRECTIONS AND CHANGES

When observing a player, you should keep in mind an order of specific checkpoints for each stroke. You must gain an eye for the important elements in a student's stroke and be able to analyze his or her technique for making corrections. It's best to keep things simple when looking for checkpoints in technique. Too much information will only confuse your students.

Below are some basic checkpoints to consider:

Stance

1. How are the student's feet placed?

2. Are the knees relaxed?

3. Is the student on his/her toes?

4. Can the student shuffle, slide and recover into the positions of hitting stances?

Grip

1. How does the student hold the racquet?

2. Does he/she choke up on the handle?

3. Is the grip loose or firm?

4. How much wrist motion is there?

5. Can the student change grips effectively?

Swing

1. What is the trajectory of the swing pattern?

2. Does the student bring the racquet back early?

3. Does the student contact out in front?

4. Is the length of follow-through correct?

Usually players attend tennis camps and clinics with the intention of making some changes in their games. Some students, however, are reluctant to make changes, feeling that they are too old to break bad habits or that their own personal style is good enough for their caliber of play. Since you will probably have the students for a relatively short period of time, you cannot expect to revise their game styles entirely. Still, their games will improve substantially if you give them enough advice and enough balls to hit. The first goal an instructor has is to improve the stroke the student uses. Work with what they have unless there is some drastically unscientific, improper element involved, in which case you will have to correct the mistake. Since people are hesitant to change, the instructor should estimate carefully when a major change should be made and if it is even possible. There should be a legitimate reason for asking the student to change. The instructor should explain the reasons to the student and remind him/her that it will take time to feel comfortable with the change. It is important to give the student easy balls to hit when he is practicing his new technique and to let him develop confidence before increasing the level of difficulty.

Many students will be taking lessons from other tennis professionals. Because of this, they may already be working to change their strokes, and you should find out if this is the case. Do your best to support their current efforts. Since tennis has generally approved techniques, most professional advice should be similar. If the student feels that there's a conflict between what has been taught to him before and what he is being taught now, do your best to clarify the discrepancy. Generally conflicts are the result of slight misunderstandings and misinterpretations. By explaining things again the problem will most likely be settled. Making sure the student has the whole story on the stroke he is trying to accomplish may eliminate what was thought to be a conflict. In any case, discuss the situation with the student and with other experienced instructors so that the information conforms to the accepted standards. Whatever is decided, remember that the student has some loyalty to his home professional, and you should not undermine that relationship or refute what his home professional has taught.

Encouraging the student to watch the ball more closely will improve contact. Encouraging the student to move into better position will enhance their balance. Encouraging the student to prepare earlier will make shots easier. All of these actions will improve the results of their swing.

WHAT YOU SAY IS IMPORTANT

Instructions must be simple, understandable and appropriate. It is one thing to read a textbook and know what it says, it is another to be able to tell a student what to do to correct his problem. When the instructor is giving directions or explanations, he must have the attention of the group. The students want to pay attention and hear what is being said, but nearby distractions may interrupt their concentration. Be patient and wait until the entire group is ready to listen before making your points. Keep your comments brief to help your students concentrate on what you say. To hold the students' interest, give them information in a style they will comprehend and enjoy. The more intelligent your speech, the more likely they will listen and pay attention. Sometimes this requires a dramatic and excited tone of voice; sometimes this requires serious convincing. The instructor should speak with confidence, and he should have confidence in the material. Humor can be a strong asset, but different people have different senses of humor, and jokes are not always taken the same way. Be sure to know the group before trying humorous comments and never make a joke at any student's expense.

Before giving instructions, make sure you have observed and understand the student's stroke. Some general advice applies to everyone and can always be offered, but to give an instruction just to say something may only confuse the player. Offer your advice sincerely and make sure the students know that your comments are serious. The comments made to the students should help them understand their strokes and make improvements. Tell them what is good in their strokes and how that affects their results. Inform the students of the science involved in tennis and how grips, swings, spins and actions fit together. Make sure the student is aware of what he is doing and what should be done to improve.

When instructing, concentrate on one item at a time. Neither instructor nor student can focus on several things at once. Give one instruction and do not give another until the student has had time to work on the first. Ask the student if he understands your advice and has any questions. Find out if he feels and sees what is supposed to be happening. Make sure he recognizes the difference between the new and the old ways of making the stroke. Many times the instructor will have to repeat the instruction to refresh the student's memory or correct the student on the proper technique. Sometimes the same basic instruction can be rephrased to give the student a different way of viewing the same thing. Picture words and phrases may make things more vivid for the student and help him improve faster.

What you say and the way you say it is important. The information given to the student must be correct. You must speak so that all who are intended to hear can hear, and you should speak clearly in a common vocabulary. You must speak at the proper rate for comprehension and be prepared to reiterate any important points. Speak in a confident and sincere tone of voice. Make sense and speak to the point.

Quite often it is best to refrain from speaking. Too much explanation may become boring. Speak at times that will not distract the students from their performance. Although it is possible to discuss a stroke while hitting, it is also possible to speak, let the student hit, and then speak again. Have a group conference for general materials; speak to individuals about personal instruction. There are many occasions for both. Speak to the group during mass drill; speak to the individuals when it is their turn to rally with you.

Speak with the students when they arrive at the court and when picking up balls. Public speaking courses are available and their basics are well-known: organize your comments, repeat important points, enunciate and pronounce properly, use modified tones for emphasis and appeal, use proper eye contact, posture and gestures. Practice giving speeches to improve delivery, memory, fluency and timing.

Where students are concerned, a verbal understanding of the stroke will assist the physical performance of the stroke. The strokes and their results follow laws which the student should know. The action in the game is logical and can be articulated. An instructor must be able to see what a player is doing and explain it well.

ORGANIZATION AND PLANNING

One of the keys to instruction is preparation. The instructor must continually work toward knowing the subject more thoroughly. Whenever teaching an assigned topic, be sure to know exactly what information is to be covered and do your best to meet the schedule. The instructor should be familiar with a number of different drills that would be applicable to the subject and the ability of the group. The instructor should have alternate drills ready in case an interruption occurs; for example, if the instructor has a ball machine drill scheduled and the machine isn't available. The instructor should also have accessory drills to develop the subject if the students make progress faster than expected.

Arrange and present drills with attention to sequence, difficulty and variety. Naturally, the better the instructor knows the groups, the more accurately he can select and use the proper drills. The instructor must stay attuned to the mood of the group and the personalities of the individual members. Take into account the students' peculiarities and commonalities. If there are people with similar problems, place them near one another so that they can work together. If there are people who would serve as good models for others, place them next to someone they can help. For strategy drills, know who are the strongest and most competitive players and make balanced teams. For example, arrange serve return drills so that the strong servers are serving to the strong returners.

To help the lesson run smoothly, it is necessary to rotate the students through various positions on the court so that everyone spends equal time with the instructor. Occasionally a student will have to change positions more quickly than might be preferred, but the welfare of the group must come first. Of course, if a student is on the verge of success, the instructor should use his discretion in keeping the student a little longer in hopes of a breakthrough. It is always possible to let the student move to the next position knowing what he must continue to work on.

There are several ways to give an individual student extra help without the group being disadvantaged. Allow the student to stand near you when he is not hitting and review the points to be emphasized. Allow the student to leave the hitting positions temporarily so that he can practice a few swings without having to strike the ball. If a student is having some difficulty, the time during the ball pick-up may give the instructor a chance to solve the problem. Take the student aside and toss a few extra balls to him or review the material. After helping the most needy, use the ball pick-up time to check with other students to find out if they have any specific questions. This time gives the instructor a chance to ask questions of the students, to give them a preview of upcoming material, or to instruct them in court etiquette.

Teamwork is very important where instructors are involved. Working with another person can be enjoyable and easy, particularly if there is cooperation and exchange between parties. Talk things over with your partner before taking the court and review topics to be considered and drills to be used.

Decide who will do what. Plan your introductions, mass drill work and class program. Exchange responsibilities. If one person explains the material and starts the class for the first period, allow the other partner a chance to do things the second period. Check quickly with one another in between periods to see if there are any special items to be remembered or any changes that should be made. Support one another. Do not contradict one another. Understand the overall goal and work toward it. Do whatever you can to support one another's efforts and to keep the class moving smoothly.

VOLUME OF TENNIS BALLS

Tennis is a game that requires a great deal of practice before it is mastered. Much of the difference between an average player and a good player stems from the difference in their experience with the game. To learn tennis, one must play tennis. That means hitting balls over and over, in different ways and from different opponents. Remember, both learning and enjoying tennis are largely dependent on the interaction of the ball and racquet. Give the students a chance to hit. Give them a chance to hit as often as possible.

Whether feeding balls, hitting or rallying, keep the tempo of the lesson brisk and the number of struck balls high. Give the students enough shots to discover the proper action and to groove it. The proper tempo of the lesson depends upon the ability and strength of the group, but when up to six people are on the court, the instructor must work hard to feed enough balls to the students to keep them all busy. The class must be energetic and lively enough for the students to feel that they are getting plenty of practice and exercise. Keep things moving and make sure the students are active and happy.

At times it is possible to explain points of mechanics or strategy while the group is hitting, and thus not break the sequence of their shot production. Naturally, for complete concentration, it would be necessary to stop all rallying and call the group together for a conference.

The more shots the students make, the more likely their muscles will become tired and need rest. After a certain period of exercise, either change the drill to emphasize another swing or change the tempo of the drill so that the students can catch their breath. It can be difficult to know the proper pace for the group. By listening to the group's breathing and watching for any noticeable weakening in their arms and legs, you should be able to know who is tiring.

By giving the students a large number of shots, you can help them see patterns in their swings and train their muscles to perform automatically. Still, a large volume of balls alone will not guarantee that the students will improve. The instructor should show exactly what to do and oversee the students' practice. Students improve at different rates, and even fast-learning students stay at a certain caliber of play for a certain time. Be patient with the students by giving them several chances to discover the shot, several more chances to know the shot, and then several chances to review the shot.

Ball machines have made it possible to practice a number of similar shots one after another. Some machines are capable of giving you a variety of shots to practice in one sequence. But ball machines have their pros and cons. Whereas they can benefit the students greatly, they can also give the students time to ingrain bad habits or misconceptions. An instructor must monitor the students working on the machine to make sure the volume of balls they're hitting are in accord with their instruction. When the students receive a volume of balls, they should also receive a volume of footwork exercise and a volume of challenge.

IMPROVING YOUR COMMUNICATION SKILLS

As a tennis instructor, every time you walk on the court you have to perform. You have to keep the interest of your students and share your tennis knowledge with them before they become bored. Your communication skills directly relate to the way people react to you. If you are unsure about your communication skills, your students will sense that and assume you are unsure about your tennis as well. This is one sure way to lose your clients. In order to increase your client list, you must improve your communication skills. To be a good communicator, I suggest you start by becoming a good listener. Listen to what your students are saying, whether you agree with them or not. You'll be able to share your expertise with your students and respond better simply by listening to what they have to say. Below are some other ways to improve your communication skills:

Be excited — A slow monotonous voice won't motivate anyone. If you expect your players to be enthusiastic and excited about learning, you must be that way yourself, especially where children are concerned. Children often judge excitement levels by our facial expressions and the tone of our voices.

Open your mouth — You need to be heard. All too often, I've seen beginning instructors try to speak without really opening their mouths. To be heard, you need to open your mouth and let the sound come out.

Pausing — Be sure to pause after each new idea. If you don't pause, your ideas may overlap each other as you are trying to make a point. Pause after each point and think about what you're trying to say before you open your mouth again. Give the listener a chance to take in what you have just said before you go on to the next point. It can also be helpful to ask for feedback after each point to make sure that the students understand.

Volume — Instructors and coaches who are always very quiet give the impression that what they have to say is of little consequence. So speak a bit more loudly than your normal voice, but don't shout.

Variety — Let your voice have variety. Be wary of a monotonous tone and allow the pitch of your voice to highlight certain words during your instruction. For example, "The trouble with your volley is that you aren't making contact out in front." The important words to emphasize are "trouble," "contact" and "front."

Part 2
Essentials of the Game

GRIPS

One of the first questions a novice tennis player asks is "How do I hold the racquet?" The four basic grips are important to know. How a player grips the racquet has a lot to do with how that player plays the game.

Each grip has specific uses to apply spins and produce power. Traditionally, the grips are called the eastern, western, continental and two-handed grips. Each grip has its benefits and limitations. For example, the continental grip can be used to hit almost every shot in tennis, but with limited power and spin. The western grip is used to impart heavy topspin on the ball, but players using this grip tend to have trouble with low bouncing balls, and miss-hits are a common occurrence due to the extreme angle of the swing pattern. I recommend that novice players begin playing the game with the eastern forehand and backhand grips because the face of the racquet is predominantly square with the ball at impact, with a relatively level swing pattern.

Eastern Grip

The most conventional of the grips is the eastern grip. To form the eastern grip, sometimes called the shake-hands grip, slide the palm of your hand down the throat and handle of the racquet, then grip and shake hands with it. Another way to get to the grip is to place the "V" created between the index finger and thumb of your racquet hand on the upper right beveled edge (for right-handed players, opposite for lefties) of the racquet handle to hit a forehand. This would be between one and two o'clock on the handle of the racquet. To get to the eastern backhand grip, simply rotate your hand about a quarter of a turn to the opposite beveled edge of the handle. This would be between 10 and 11 o'clock on the grip for right-handed players and between one and two o'clock for lefties. You must switch

Eastern grip

your grips to utilize the eastern grips appropriately. If you use the forehand grip to hit a backhand, the head of your racquet will be tilted too much to meet the ball squarely at impact. One of the benefits of using the eastern grip for your ground strokes is that you can use a variety of spins on your shots.

Western Grip

The more extreme of the grips is the western grip. It is generally used by more advanced players who want to hit high looping shots with excessive topspin. With this grip, the racquet hand is even farther behind the handle than it is with the eastern grip. Place the "V" created between the index finger and thumb on the right or left beveled edge of

Western grip

the racquet handle. This would be about three o'clock for a right-hander's forehand and about nine o'clock for a lefty's forehand. To hit backhand, it would be the opposite.

I don't recommend the western grip to beginner or intermediate players because it is difficult to meet the ball squarely at impact. The swing pattern is too extreme. To execute consistent ground strokes using this grip, a player must possess a strong wrist and excellent timing.

Continental Grip

The continental grip can be used in the execution of any basic shot in tennis, including the serve, volley, overhead smash and all ground strokes. Although this grip is obviously very versatile, it lacks the ability to produce increased power and topspin on ground strokes. The continental grip can be used effectively to impart underspin on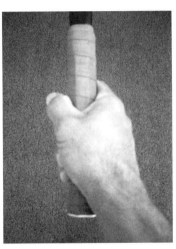

Continental grip

ground strokes and to hit volleys without having to change the grip. This is an excellent grip for beginners to use for the simple reason that they don't have to change their grip while playing a point. As their skills improve, they should try other grips that will allow them to hit more spins with power, accuracy and control.

Two-Handed Grip

The two-handed grip is generally used for the backhand side only. Although it is possible to use two hands off both sides, it's difficult to switch grips from forehand to backhand. The two-handed grip is accomplished by placing the dominant hand on the bottom of the handle and the nondominant hand above it. The nondominant hand should be in an eastern forehand position, while the dominant hand can be in any position that is comfortable to you. I recommend a continental position for the dominant hand.

STANCES

Ready stance

Ready Stance

How a player stands when he or she is waiting for the opponent to hit the ball has an enormous impact on the player's shot-making abilities and effectiveness. For the ready stance, a player should stand with his racquet out in front of his body, lean slightly forward with his knees flexed, and evenly distribute his body weight on the balls of his feet. I can't stress enough the importance of teaching your students to get into a ready stance when waiting for their opponents to hit the ball back to their side of the net. The ready stance keeps a player poised to move in any direction and ready to react to any shot the opponent might hit.

Hitting Stance

After a player has moved into the general area of the ball, he or she needs to assume a stance that will provide a solid foundation from which to hit. A hitting stance is accomplished by turning the shoulders, bringing the racquet back, and supporting the body weight on the rear foot. From this position, a player is poised to begin the forward swing and make contact with the ball. This stance allows a player to regain or maintain balance and control of movement before beginning the forward swing. There are three basic hitting stances to choose from when hitting either forehands or backhands.

Closed stance

Closed Stance

Traditionally, the closed stance is taught to beginners because it allows a player to step into the shot as he or she begins to make a forward swing at the ball. From this stance, it's easy to transfer the body weight from the rear foot to the front foot, making it easier to gain forward momentum.

Open Stance

More and more tennis instructors are teaching the open stance in favor of the closed stance. It's easier to hit heavy topspin shots off the forehand using an open stance. Hitting from an open stance also starts the recovery process earlier during the follow-through. Because the player is not exactly stepping into the shot, power comes from an aggressive hips-waist-and-shoulder-turn while making contact with the ball well out in front and to the right of the body.

Open stance

Neutral stance

Neutral Stance

Most intermediate and advanced players adopt a stance between the open and closed stances out of necessity and convenience. The neutral stance is more versatile. From this stance, a player can make adjustments in his or her swing if a bad bounce or last-second decision to change shots occurs. With this stance, players can also use any grip they want effectively and hit any shot in the book with equal ease.

Although all of the stances should be in a player's arsenal, I recommend that instructors teach the neutral stance for executing all ground strokes, forehands or backhands, to all students relatively new to tennis.

FOOTWORK AND MOVEMENT

During the course of a tennis match, how much time is actually spent swinging at and striking the ball? It only takes a second or two to bring the racquet back and begin to swing forward to make contact with the ball. Even if the match is a marathon lasting three or four hours, only a few minutes are spent actually hitting the ball. What is a player doing the rest of the time? You guessed it: running and moving to get into position to hit the next shot. That is the reason movement and footwork are so important. Good footwork is the solid foundation upon which all ground strokes are built. What good is a powerful forehand if a player can't get to the ball or is out of position and off balance when making contact with the ball?

Footwork and movement are related, but they're not the same thing. Movement is the act of getting from one general area of the court to the other. Footwork is the adjustment a player makes with his feet when getting into the general area of the ball and preparing to hit a shot. I've listed and illustrated seven key steps to improve movement and footwork to help your players get into position to hit some killer ground strokes.

Thrust

A player's movement toward the ball is only as effective as the initial step. When the player decides in which direction he needs to go to get to the ball, he must pivot off his inside foot and push off with his outside foot. This movement also turns the hips and shoulders to begin racquet preparation.

Adjustment Steps

If a player is on the run, he is obviously taking large steps to get into position to hit the ball. As he gets closer to the oncoming ball, he must take smaller adjustment steps to maintain balance and control of his movement before she begins her forward swing and makes contact with the ball.

Plant

With early racquet preparation, teach your players to support their body weight with the rear leg by firmly planting the rear foot behind as they complete the backswing. The plant will allow your student to remain balanced when shifting the weight from the rear foot to the front foot, creating an opportunity to put some weight into his shot. Forehand or backhand, be sure your students are getting good shoulder and hip rotation while bringing their racquets back to establish a solid foundation from which to hit.

Drop and Recover

After hitting the ball, a player has to recover for the next shot. Hanging around and admiring a shot will get any player into trouble, so teach students to get ready to move. When they have to change direction to get to the opponent's oncoming ball, they must drop the center of the body core for balance, pivot off the inside foot, and push off with the outside foot. Completing the stroke with a full follow-through and allowing the racquet to come across the front of the body will begin the recovery process.

Crossover Steps

If a player has to cover some ground without breaking into a dead run, the fastest and most efficient way to recover is by repeatedly crossing the trailing foot over the lead foot until he has established decent court positioning.

Shuffle Steps

If a player is severely out of position and the opponent hits the ball in the opposite corner, the player is going to have to run to recover. If a player is moderately out of position, he should use crossover steps to improve his court position. In either case, a player can use smaller shuffle steps to gain final positioning when establishing the hitting stance. Even if a player doesn't have to change court position at all, a shuffle step should be taken to get off the heels and in position to adjust to the oncoming ball's bounce.

Split-Step

After a player has established a good court position and is in a ready stance, the split-step can be used just as the opponent starts to hit the ball. The split is a little hop coming down with the weight evenly distributed on the balls of the feet. The split-step is usually used after a player has established good court positioning, when returning a serve, or when preparing to hit a volley. At the end of the split, the player should be leaning slightly forward, with the racquet placed comfortably out in front of the body.

GROUND STROKES

Forehand Drive

For most players the forehand is the shot that they can count on when the rest of their game falls apart. A stroke to call on at critical times during the course of a match, the forehand is the big weapon. Most players learn the forehand first because it's a familiar motion to them. Since childhood, the acts of throwing a ball, swinging a baseball bat, or rolling a bowling ball have become familiar motions that all relate to the forehand in some way or another. The instrument or object is taken back behind you in a backswing fashion and re-leased or thrown by stepping in or leaning in with your body. At any rate, I recommend that all beginners learn

Forehand drive

the forehand first. It's important to learn the stroke properly from the start to avoid slipping into bad habits as the novice's game develops.

Slice Forehand

The slice forehand seems to be a forgotten shot in today's modern game, especially when hit from the baseline. Professional players rarely use the slice forehand, except when they're out of court position and in trouble. The ideal time to hit a shot with underspin is when an opponent has hit a ball landing short on your player's side of the net. This gives a player the opportunity to attack by hitting a shot with underspin to keep the ball low, denying the opponent a good look at a passing shot. There are several different situations in

Slice forehand

which a player would benefit by hitting a slice forehand. For example, if the opponent uses heavy topspins on his ground strokes, it's a good idea to return spin with spin. By hitting the shot with underspin, your player will keep the ball spinning in the same direction, giving him added control. More often than not, most players who hit heavy topspin shots will have trouble returning balls hit with underspin because the ball has a lower bounce.

I recommend that you teach your players to use a continental forehand grip to hit the slice forehand. The execution of this shot is similar to the forehand drive, except that the racquet is taken back to about shoulder height during the backswing and remains there until your students begin their forward swing downward to make contact with the ball.

Two-Handed Backhand

Wherever people are playing tennis, from the public parks to the professional stadiums and arenas, you'll see people of all ages using two hands on the backhand side. The two-handed backhand boom is here to stay. Back in the 1940s, players such as Pancho Segura came onto the scene using two hands in a professional atmosphere for the first time. Since then, we've seen a significant number of pros rise to the top using two hands on the backhand side: Chris Evert, Jimmy Connors, Bjorn Borg, Andre Agassi, and the list goes on. Today's teaching pros are following suit.

The majority of today's youngsters start out hitting two-handed backhands. I started out using two hands on the backhand side because I needed the other hand on the racquet for more power and control. Although I switched to a one-handed backhand as I got older and stronger, many players continue to use the two-handed backhand throughout their careers.

Two-handed backhand

While the two-handed backhand can be a powerful weapon, it has its limitations. A player's reach is limited in some situations, and it can be difficult to get out of the way of a ball coming right at you. Even if your students prefer the two-handed shot, I recommend teaching them a one-handed shot so that they have extra reach for wide balls.

One great plus for the two-handed backhand is that you can disguise the direction of your shots with a flick of the wrists. Racquet technology and athletic conditioning have raised the level of all shot-making in tennis, contributing to the effectiveness of the two-handed shot.

Backhand Drive

Some teaching professionals believe the one-handed backhand drive is a relatively easy ground stroke to learn because it's a natural movement. The hitting arm opens up to the court during the forward swing to make contact with the ball, as opposed to closing off to the court when hitting the forehand. Although this is true, the one-handed backhand can be a difficult shot to hit for some players. Some players lack the arm and wrist strength to pull the racquet through. The way to remedy this is to have students practice their timing. By improving their timing, the players don't necessarily need to have a great deal of arm strength.

Good timing begins with the shoulder turn. Don't allow your students to just move their racquet to the

Backhand drive

backhand side with their arms; have them turn side-ways with a step and rotate their shoulders to get the racquet moving back. Be sure they get their racquets back all the way in one smooth motion without exaggeration. To practice timing from this point, use what I call the "timing tool." As the player begins his forward swing, tell him to say to himself, "Bounce and step and hit." Saying this out loud or in the mind in a normal tone and speed will get the timing of the swing in sync. Your players can use this tool in the execution of all ground strokes. If they have to run to get into position, they should simply wait until they've established a good hitting stance before they say it.

Slice Backhand

Most players who use a one-handed backhand have some variety in their shots off that side. Usually the

Slice backhand

variety includes a slice backhand. The slice backhand is one of the most natural strokes in tennis. Bringing the racquet back to shoulder-height position on the backswing is as natural as blinking the eyes. The trick is in knowing what to do with the racquet from that position. Most beginners chop down at the ball, giving it too much spin and causing it to float or pop up in the air with little or no pace. The slice backhand is accomplished by having the racquet head tilted at impact instead of swinging at the ball with a severely angled trajectory. The slice backhand may be used for deep penetrating shots or to create angles to move the opponent around the court. The slice backhand can also be used to attack the net. The underspin created by slicing the ball keeps the ball low on its bounce, making it a little more difficult for the opponent to hit.

FUNDAMENTALS FOR BETTER GROUND STROKES

Use an eastern grip – The racquet head is relatively square with the ball at impact when using an eastern grip.

Be ready to move – A player must assume a ready stance and be prepared to move quickly either sideways for wide balls or toward the net for shorter balls. Good footwork is the solid foundation upon which all ground strokes are built. A powerful forehand is useless if the player can't get to the ball or if he is out of position and off balance when making contact with the ball.

Turn the shoulders – The most common mistake players make on their ground strokes is not getting their racquets back quickly enough. As soon as a player realizes that he is about to hit a ground

Turn your shoulders.

stroke, he must turn the upper body to get the racquet moving. As he begins the backswing, he begins stepping or running into position to make the shot. A player must take a full backswing and not a half-hearted one. A full backswing permits a full swing at the ball.

Step out to meet the ball – To hit powerful ground strokes, a player must put his weight into the shot. He can only do that by stepping out to meet the ball as it comes toward his racquet. He then turns sideways to the ball as he takes his racquet back and plants his body weight on his rear foot. Teach your players to step toward the ball as they start their forward swing, transferring weight into their shots.

Up and through – Since most ground strokes are made close to or behind the baseline, the ball will have to travel nearly the full length of the court to get

Step out to meet the ball: forehand

Step out to meet the ball: backhand

the kind of depth it should. To ensure this, your students must bring their racquet up from a low to high position to meet the ball.

Keep the ball on the strings at impact – Your students should make contact with the ball just in front of the forward foot and keep the ball on the strings as long as possible. The racquet face should travel on a straight upward line through the hitting zone in the direction you want the ball to go. Accuracy will increase if the ball is kept on the strings by driving the racquet through the ball and not at it. As a player hits through the ball, his weight should move forward to add extra power to the shot. This is called weight transfer.

Meet the ball firmly – Many novice players try to get rid of the ball as quickly as possible. Instead of hitting through the ball, they slap or swat at it using lots of wrist action. When hitting ground strokes, the wrist and forearm should move as one unit until the ball leaves the racquet. This will help players meet the ball firmly and will give them more control.

Concentrate on the hitting zone – The most critical part of any ground stroke is the hitting zone where your racquet contacts the ball. For most players, the hitting zone starts in front of the hip and continues to where the racquet is almost parallel with the front foot and above the knees. As mentioned, the objective should be to keep the ball on the strings for as much of that hitting zone as possible. Your students need to concentrate on the ball and watch it in the hitting zone.

Follow-through – As a player completes the stroke, he must follow through as far out in front as pos-

Follow-through: forehand   *Follow-through: backhand*

sible. A full follow-through will ensure that he hits through the ball and maintains the speed of the racquet head until the ball leaves the strings. It will also help your students complete the weight transfer and finish with all their weight on their front foot. During practice, have them freeze their position at the end of their stroke to ensure a complete and full follow-through.

Get to the ball quickly – Getting to the ball is half the battle in tennis. If your students can reach the ball in plenty of time, they can prepare for the shot, hit the ball smoothly and recover easily for the next shot. The first step toward the ball should be a thrust to move in the right direction. Teach them to skip or use shuffle steps to get within one stride of hitting the ball, then plant their foot and step into the shot.

FUNDAMENTALS OF NET PLAY

To volley means to stand at the net and hit the ball before it bounces. Naturally, players don't start out at the net unless playing doubles. If playing singles, a player will have to transition from the baseline to the net. This is accomplished in several different ways. During the course of a rally from the baseline, the opponent may hit a drop shot to bring a player to the net, or the player may have an aggressive game attacking the net. In either case, the player is at the net. What to do now? First of all, the player must not panic. If he tries to return to the baseline, he'll only get caught in the middle of the court. This no-man's land is a vulnerable court position. Instead, teach him to stand his ground and prepare to volley.

A player must be taught to use a grip that will work off both sides. Since your student will be closer to the opponent, he won't have a lot of time to prepare. Trying to change his grip from forehand to backhand could be a handicap. I recommend teaching your students to use the continental grip. With this grip, they can hit off both sides without changing.

Their second concern should be to remember not to take a full backswing in preparing to hit a volley. A full backswing could cause them to be late making contact with the ball. The volley is a short, quick stroke that should be executed almost instinctively. Net play is usually fast-paced action, so it should be kept simple.

Many club and weekend players have poor volleys because they believe it's a shot they don't have to practice. On the contrary, not practicing volleys can be disastrous. Missing the easy put-away is embarrassing, so make your students practice their volleys and keep it short and simple.

Use one grip at the net – The continental grip is recommended for net play because the pace of play

Wait with your racquet up.

is so fast. However, your players may find it easier to volley using eastern grips off both sides, forehand and backhand, in the early learning stages. I recommend that novices switch grips in the beginning. As their skills progress, they can adopt a continental grip to get to the next level of play.

Wait with the racquet up – Teach students to wait with the racquet head up and out in front when playing at the net. It's important to keep the racquet head up because most of the balls volleyed will be at net height or higher. To volley a low ball, a player must bend the knees to get down to the level of the ball and execute the volley properly.

Turn the shoulders to bring the racquet to the side – Because time is so short at the net, players should use little or no backswing when hitting a volley. From the ready position, they should turn the

Forehand volley   *Backhand volley*

Step toward the ball.

racquet so that the strings face the ball. The next step is to bring the racquet to meet the ball. As volleying skills improve, your students can take short backswings by turning their shoulders and opening the face of the racquet, holding it high. If you find that they are not timing their volleys well, have them shorten their backswing again until they are meeting the ball squarely.

Step toward the ball – When players have enough time, they should move toward the ball as they hit the volleys. Being in the right place is half the game when volleying. They should take short rapid steps to get close to the ball and make the final step with the foot farthest from the ball. The last step will allow players to stretch out for the ball. This move is called "cutting the ball off." Teach them to move their weight into the shot to give it a little extra punch. This will help them to be properly balanced and ready to recover for the next shot.

Move in and hit the ball out in front – Players should be taught to meet the ball out in front of them. Not only can they see the ball better, but they'll be able to hit the ball more sharply by moving in. And although they'll sacrifice power by hitting the ball well out in front, almost all the power they'll need will be supplied by the pace of their opponent's shot. As they hit their volley, their forearm and elbow should move forward together. Even though they employ a short forward swing on the volley, they'll get plenty of power into the shot if they use their body weight and keep a firm wrist and grip.

Watch the ball intently – I can never emphasize too much the importance of keeping the eyes on the

Move in and hit the ball out in front.

ball, especially when at the net. Teach your players to focus on the ball because there is so little time to react, and any lapse of concentration could be disastrous.

Keep the follow-through short – The punching action on the volley should be short follow-through. Players should simply let the racquet head continue after the ball in the direction they wish to send it. A short follow-through will help place the ball accurately, and a long follow-through won't add anything to the shot. The racquet should follow the ball's direction briefly and then come back quickly to get into the ready position for the next shot.

DEVELOPING A CONSISTENT SERVE

The serve is probably the most important shot in tennis. It is also one of the most difficult shots to learn to hit properly. For some players, hitting the ball when it's over their head can be difficult to time. Tossing the ball in the air with one hand, while transferring body weight and simultaneously taking the racquet back, around, up and through to make contact with the ball is a lot of movement to synchronize. The serve should be practiced religiously so that it can be hit consistently. When the serve is executed properly, it can be a lethal weapon. On the other hand, it can also ruin a player's game. It's the one shot the player is totally in control of. So when it gets messed up, there's only one person to blame.

Pace, direction, placement and spin are all variables that give the server the advantage when beginning a point. The receiver is left wondering about these variables when his opponent steps up to the service line and begins to set up to hit the serve. When serving, it is always a good tactic to keep the opponent guessing. Teach your students to mix it up a little. Changing the speed of the serve from time to time, as well as the placement and spin, will keep an opponent on his toes. A player should try to serve to his opponent's weaknesses.

Step 1: The Toss

The first step in serving is the ball toss, the act of consistently tossing the ball in the contact zone. A student might ask, "What's so hard about tossing a ball in the air and then hitting it?" Nothing really. A player just has to serve the ball in a way that is not going to leave him vulnerable. There's nothing worse than hitting a cream puff serve and watching the opponent wind up to annihilate it. This is just one of the reasons that students should develop a consistent ball toss before moving on to the second part of this lesson.

Have them start out by stepping up to the service line and standing perpendicular to the net. Then have them place the ball in the fingertips of their nondominant hand and practice tossing the ball in the air. Get their arms moving and extending upward to release the ball. They should create some momentum with their movement. Without letting the ball roll off the end of their fingers, they must extend their arms upward and open their hands, releasing the ball. The toss should be out over the court and a little to the right. Have them toss the ball high enough to get full extension at impact. It's a good idea for students to practice this many times before attempting a full serve.

Step 2: The Serve

> *Ready* — Players must step up to the service line and get comfortable. Have them take a deep breath and think about what they're doing. They

Ready

Open

Backscratch

Contact

should begin by aligning their feet properly. Feet are about shoulder-width apart, with the lead foot at a 45-degree angle to the baseline. The rear foot should be parallel to the baseline. The body is perpendicular to the net, with both arms out in front.

Open – The body weight is resting on the rear foot. Arms are open and weight is shifted forward. The racquet is brought down by the legs as the player begins to move the ball-arm upward for the toss.

Backscratch – As the ball leaves the hand, your student should continue shifting his weight forward as he brings the racquet to a "back-scratching position." He then extends to release the ball and keeps his head up.

Contact – Using the legs to push off and trying to become fully extended at impact, your student should snap the wrist and rotate the shoulders to get more power on the serve. The contact zone should be out over the court as high as he can reach.

Follow-through – During the follow-through, the player must allow the racquet to come across the body, down by the legs, to ensure a complete stroke. The head should be kept up throughout the entire stroke.

Follow-through

Recover – To recover, the player continues the follow-through all the way across the body. The student then ends up in a ready stance.

RETURNING SERVE

If the serve is the most important shot in tennis, then getting it back is the next priority. The service return is not just another ground stroke. Matches are won and lost with service returns. If the opponent has a booming serve, this is when a player is most vulnerable. Developing a consistent service return is crucial. The first step in developing a consistent return is to get organized. Before your students step up to the line to return serve, have them walk around the baseline area to get their thoughts together. They should consider the score, choose a grip, take notice of where the opponent has been serving, do anything to develop a consistent routine. It also helps to have in mind a specific area of the court to hit to. Doing this will help your students relax and improve their shot-making. Another key is to get the racquet moving. The ball is going to be on top of the receiver quickly, so getting the racquet to the appropriate side immediately is key.

This brings up the issue of the backswing. A player should turn his shoulders but take a shorter backswing if his opponent has a fast serve. Most club and weekend players make the mistake of taking a big backswing, causing them to be late making contact with the ball. Teach your students to develop a "chip shot" when returning against big servers. The chip is almost like hitting a volley, except it is hit off the bounce. Finally, players should stay down when returning serve. There should be no wasted motion. Bend the knees and stay on the same horizontal plane as the approaching ball and forward swing. As with the volley, the player's eyes should be near the level of the ball, so he can focus on the point of contact.

Set and Split

When setting the stance and preparing to return serve, your students should have a wide, balanced foundation with their feet about shoulder-width apart and their weight leaning slightly forward. They should start a step or two behind the baseline so they can move forward into a split-step just as the opponent hits a serve. The split will get players ready to move in any direction.

Choose Grip and Move Racquet Back

Once it is determined which side the opponent has served to, a player must choose his grip while turning sideways. He should use the shoulders to get the racquet moving back. At this point, your students should have in mind a particular area of the court they would like the return to go to.

Cut Off

It's a good idea not to take a full backswing. By short-ening the back-swing, players increase the odds of making solid contact out in front. During the backswing, a player should step or shuffle into position and plant his weight on his rear foot to establish his balance. Then, from a good hitting foundation, the player can step forward with the lead foot to cut off the oncoming ball.

Stay Down

There should be no wasted motion on the return serve. At impact, the player must stay down and transfer his weight into the shot. The result of staying down and leaning into the shot will be a more powerful and controlled return.

Set and split

Cut off

Stay down

Follow-through

Follow Through

Teach your students to stay with their shot and complete the follow-through to keep the ball on the strings longer. They must extend outward toward the target area. Teach them to keep it simple. They don't need to overcomplicate the follow-through with excessive movement.

Recover

A long follow-through will facilitate the recovery process. The rear leg comes around, and the player can pivot off the inside foot while pushing off the outside foot to begin recovery. Shuffle or cross-over steps may be used to get back into position. The player should assume a ready stance when he has established a good court position.

THE OVERHEAD SMASH

The overhead smash is not really a difficult shot to hit, but some beginner, intermediate and club players manage to make it appear that way. Usually, missing an overhead is caused by overhitting or by being out of position. Like the serve, the overhead smash should be a controlled shot, not hit exclusively with power but also with direction and placement. Trying to blast the shot can result in an embarrassing miss or a severe mishit.

Think of the overhead smash as a serve with footwork. In fact, if a player has an adequate serve, he can develop a reliable overhead that won't let him down in the critical stages of a match. Usually the opportunity for hitting an overhead smash comes at the net, when an opponent tries to lob the ball over a player's head.

The overhead smash can be played out of the air or sometimes off the bounce. There are appropriate times for doing either. For example, if your student can manage to hit the ball out of the air, he should do so, because he'll be taking court away from his opponent and giving him less time to react. On the other hand, there are times when he should let the ball bounce in order to get into a better position to hit an overhead. Teach players to shuffle or cross-step back and let the ball bounce, giving themselves more time to get into position. In either situation, when a player sees that his opponent has hit a lob, his first instinct should be to get back into position and keep the ball in front of him. Teach students to decide whether they can hit the smash out of the air, or let it bounce and try not to let the ball get behind them. It's a good idea to use the free hand and arm to point at the oncoming ball as a player brings the racquet back with a shoulder turn. The head should be kept up, and the feet should move.

Ready

The player is at the net. He must be prepared to hit a volley or an overhead. He won't know until his opponent hits a lob that he needs to move back for an overhead smash. Your student should stand with his weight slightly forward, poised on the balls of the feet with the racquet held up in front of him.

Turn Sideways

When the opponent hits a lob, the player turns sideways. The player turns his shoulders and begins to get his racquet back.

Shuffle and Point

Keeping the ball in front of his body, your student should use shuffle steps to move into position while pointing at the oncoming ball. He must try to get back quickly so that he doesn't have to leap into the air to make contact with the ball.

Ready

Turn sideways

Shuffle and point

Adjust and swing

61

Adjust and Swing

Players must establish a foundation from which to hit by adjusting the feet. The body weight is planted on the rear foot while completing the backswing. To begin the forward swing, the weight should be transferred forward by stepping into the shot with the lead foot. The racquet is brought up from a back-scratching position to make contact with the ball out in front.

Follow-Through

It is important to emphasize that students need to keep the head up during the follow-through. Many club players bring their heads down, causing them to hit the shot poorly. During the follow-through, players should get full extension out toward the target, keeping the ball on the strings longer for more control. To

Follow-through

complete the follow-through, teach students to allow the racquet to travel down by their legs.

Recover

During the follow-through, players should bring the rear leg around to facilitate the recovery process and allow them to get back into a ready stance.

USING THE LOB

The lob is one of the most underestimated and underused shots in tennis. Its effectiveness is rarely appreciated. There are several different situations that that are prime times to use the lob. To help your students utilize the lob, I'll describe some of these situations and provide a description of the mechanics of the stroke.

In the first situation, have your student imagine that he is severely out of court position, and his opponent has him on the run. This would be a good time for him to throw up a lob to give himself time to regain his court position. He must hit the ball as high as he possibly can, while keeping it in play to give himself plenty of time to get back into the point.

Another opportune time to use the lob is when the opponent is constantly rushing the net. Your student doesn't need to have a lot of height on his lob in this situation. He just needs to get his lob over his opponent's reach. Throwing up a lob from time to time can and will discourage the opponent from coming in so frequently. The lob can also be used in helping to tire an opponent out. Hitting overhead after overhead can burn up a lot of the opponent's energy. Even if the opponent realizes what your student is doing and lets the ball drop so that the opponent can hit ground strokes, he will have to generate all the pace on his shot, giving your student an advantage in the long run. Tell your students to keep in mind that the lob is not only to be used for defensive purposes, it can also be a formidable offensive weapon as well.

Disguise

Teach students not to give away the fact that they are going to hit a lob. Disguising the lob attempt can be advantageous in completing a successful lob. To disguise a lob, students will prepare as they would for a ground stroke.

Disguise

Weight Forward

Many club players make the mistake of leaning back when hitting the lob. Doing this will cause the lob to land short, giving the opponent an easy putaway. To control the ball, players should keep their weight moving forward when hitting a lob.

Weight forward

Contact

Players should swing as if hitting a ground stroke. Just before contact, they must drop the level of their racquet below the level of the ball and tilt the racquet slightly. Keeping the wrist firm will control the lift of the ball.

Contact

Follow-through

Follow-Through

Teach players to lean into their shot and use a complete follow-through to ensure depth and accuracy on the lob.

Recovery

Players can simply recover into a good court position or choose to take advantage of the opponent's position by coming into the net if the lob gets over his head.

THE DROP SHOT

The drop shot is a relatively soft shot that travels with a low trajectory. It barely clears the net and lands very short on the opponent's side of the net. Many players mistakenly think that the drop shot should be an outright winner. Realistically speaking, the drop shot should be thought of as a set-up stroke. It's meant to draw a weak reply from the opponent, putting him in a vulnerable situation. A low-bouncing shot, the drop shot should only give the opponent the opportunity to hit up on the ball while drawing him closer to the net. A high-bouncing dropper will give the opponent an opportunity to drive down on the ball, resulting in a winner.

I recommend that the drop shot be hit with underspin. Putting underspin on the drop shot will cause the ball to bite the court a little and stop the forward momentum of its flight. But warn your students to be careful: attempting to apply too much underspin can cause the shot to pop up. This gives the opponent plenty of time to run down the drop shot and puts a player in a vulnerable position. Choosing the right time to attempt a drop shot is crucial. Players should only try hitting the drop shot from inside the baseline.

All too often I see club players attempting drop shots from behind the baseline. This is difficult to accomplish for two reasons. First, being too far away from the net makes the shot difficult to execute. Second, the ball has to travel so far that the opponent has time to read the shot and effectively retrieve it. The best time to attempt

Disguise   *Step forward*

a drop shot is when a player is inside the baseline, and the opponent is behind it. The drop shot is another one of those shots that players neglect to practice. To practice, start your students out by having them hit drop shots from about the service line. As they develop some confidence, they can move farther back and bounce the ball shorter in their opponents' court.

Disguise

Have them set up as if they were hitting a ground stroke. I recommend that students set up their attempts by hitting some slice forehands and backhands at the beginning of the match. Doing this will help disguise the fact that they plan to use some drop shots.

Step Forward

It's important that the drop shot resemble the look of a normal ground stroke. Players should swing on a

Contact

downward plane to meet the ball as they step forward into the shot, just as if they were hitting a forehand or backhand slice.

Contact

While focusing on the point of contact, players should meet the ball with the racquet head tilted a little to impart underspin on the shot. They must push the racquet through as if they were hitting a volley, so the ball doesn't pop off the strings. Doing this will give more control of the shot.

Follow-Through

Players should keep the follow-through short, but longer than that of a volley. The racquet should be allowed to continue out toward the target area. Tell students to remember that they are drawing their opponent closer in, so they must begin recovery as soon as possible.

Follow-through

Recover

Once a player hits the drop shot, he may choose to follow to the net to cut off his opponent's reply, or he may choose to backpedal into a better position. Don't allow students to just hang around to see if their opponent gets to the drop shot; tell them to take advantage of the situation.

HITTING AN APPROACH SHOT

What is an approach shot? It is any shot hit from inside the baseline in an attempt to get to the net and make an offensive stand. The first and most important factor in hitting a well-executed approach shot is choosing the appropriate ball to come in on. In order to attack the net safely, your student should wait until the opponent hits a shot that lands well inside the baseline. If a player tries to attack and hit an approach shot from too deep in the court, he might be giving his opponent

69

an excellent opportunity to pass at the net. For inter-mediate and club players, I recommend that they are taught to wait until the opponent's shot lands inside the service line before they attempt an approach shot.

When hitting an approach shot, the target area should be deep in an opponent's court, near the baseline. It's a good idea to hit the approach shots down the line instead of crosscourt for a couple of reasons: the angle of the opponent's passing shot is reduced, and the ball travels in the air a shorter amount of time, giving the opponent less time to react. But it's not writ-ten in stone that a player should hit approach shots down the line. An opponent could be out of position, giving a player an open court to hit into with a crosscourt approach. In any case, the fundamentals of hitting an approach shot are basically like those of a ground stroke, only with a shorter backswing. Tell students to remem-ber that they are closer to the net than they would be during a baseline rally, so they don't need to hit a full ground stroke to have an effective approach. Have them lower the risk of overhitting by making a more con-trolled swing and taking a shorter backswing.

Like all shots in tennis, focus should be on the point of contact. In this case, students especially want to make sure they're making contact well out in front and stay-ing with their shot for pinpoint accuracy. It's important that they don't rush themselves when making an ap-proach shot. Once they see that the opponent has hit a ball landing short on their side off the net, and they've made a decision to come to the net, they must immedi-ately move forward and take the racquet back. Teach students to take their time in producing the stroke, and, since they've made the commitment to come in, they should keep moving after hitting the shot.

When they are watching the pros, ask students to

notice that the pros run through their approach shots. This is an acquired skill. Hitting on the move requires excellent timing and can be learned with practice.

Commit

Once a player has decided to hit an approach shot, he must not hesitate. He must begin by moving forward and preparing his racquet.

Short Backswing

By keeping the backswing short, a player has more control of his movement. This will enable him to make a more controlled swing.

Contact

Teach players to make contact a little farther out in front than they would for a normal ground stroke. They should stay with the shot and keep the ball on the strings longer for control.

Short backswing   *Contact*

Follow-through *Split step*

Follow-Through

Tell students to remember that they've made a commitment, so they must keep moving after hitting the ball. A long follow-through out toward the target will facilitate forward movement toward the net.

Split-Step

If the approach isn't a winning shot, a player must prepare to hit a volley or get back for an overhead. I recommend that students take a split-step just as the opponent hits the ball in order to be ready to move in any direction.

EXECUTING THE HALF-VOLLEY

What is a half-volley? It is not a volley, nor is it a full-fledged ground stroke, even though it is hit off the bounce. Usually the half-volley is used when the ball bounces almost at a player's feet. Tell students to imagine themselves in transition, trying to get to the net from the baseline. They've just hit an approach shot, and they are closing in to get to the net. Suddenly the opponent hits a shot that just clears the net. Your students aren't close enough to hit a volley before it bounces, and they aren't back far enough to hit a ground stroke. What should they do? Since the ball is literally at their feet, they have to get the racquet down to the level of the ball. This means a player has to bend his knees and upper body to get the racquet head low enough to make solid contact. If he just sticks the racquet head down there to make contact, it will be difficult to control the shot. He must bend down far enough to get the racquet hand and the racquet itself on the same horizontal plane. There's virtually no backswing with the half-volley. A player gets down, taking the racquet to either the forehand or backhand side, keeps the racquet in a parallel position to the court and simply blocks the ball with a firm grip and wrist. For a good solid half-volley, tell players to try to make contact with the ball immediately after the bounce. It is important for the players to keep moving after hitting the ball.

Although the half-volley is often a defensive shot that a player is forced to use, don't let that keep your students from taking the offensive. After the half-volley, teach players to continue up toward the net so that their next shot will be a conventional volley. If a player hits a good half-volley, body momentum will carry him forward after he hits the ball. Even the fastest players can be under pressure when forced to hit the half-volley. When under this pressure, players should concentrate on getting their hand down by bending the knees and keeping the racquet head up. Be sure your students know to grip the racquet tightly and keep a firm wrist to hit the ball firmly. The sooner they can take the ball

Commit

Short backswing

Contact

Follow-through

off the bounce, the better their half-volley will be.

Commit

Once a player commits to getting to the net, he must not stop his forward movement. When he sees that his opponent has hit a ball that's going to be at his feet, he should keep moving while getting down to the level of the oncoming ball.

Short Backswing

The ball is going to be at the player's feet quickly, so he must keep the backswing short. A player must get the racquet to the appropriate side, firm up his grip, and get ready to punch the ball as soon as it bounces in front of him.

Contact

At impact, the racquet should be tilted a little to lift the ball over the net. The point of contact should be just in front of the lead knee. Tell students to keep moving forward as they make contact.

Follow-Through

The follow-through for the half-volley is essentially the same as the follow-through for a conventional volley. Emphasize that students are on their way to the net, so follow-through should be short. They must keep moving.

Split-Step

Once the half-volley has cleared the net, and the opponent is about to make

Split-step

an attempt at passing the player at the net, he should shuffle in a little closer to the net and into a split-step. The split will get him ready to move in any direction.

Part 3
Working With Juniors

PLAYER DEVELOPMENT

The developmental approach is a term professional coaches use when working with young players. It suggests that children go through stages of development. The concept of developmental coaching means that coaches need to understand how each stage in a player's development leads to the next. When focusing on development, the key is to design a good plan for the entire year that includes a balance of training, competition and rest. As young players develop and acquire solid fundamentals, it becomes the responsibility of a coach to help guide them in the development of their skills. That plan of development must be consistent with their personalities as well as their physical, mental, technical and tactical abilities. In the development of competitive players, start by taking each player's physical and mental attributes into consideration.

Physical factors

- Height and weight

- Muscular strength and its development

- Balance, speed, agility, coordination

Mental factors

- Personality

- Patience level

- Style of play the player enjoys

While considering these factors, the coach should also take into account the three phases of development, which are as follows:

Introduction – During this phase, it's essential that a player develops the ABCs of athleticism (agility, balance and coordination) as well as the basic fundamentals of footwork, movement, stroke production and swing patterns.

Refinement – During this phase, the player plays tennis to become a better tennis player, not just to have fun. Refinement of skills, on-court decision-making and weapon development are the focal points in this stage.

Performance – This is the competitive phase and is marked by many hours of practice honing technical and tactical skills and working toward personal excellence while playing at a high level of performance.

PERIODIZATION

Success doesn't come cheap. Sure, some players are born with certain physical attributes that give them an edge in becoming better players. But how do the rest of us get to the next level?

Winning is a challenging and demanding occasion for the average junior as well as for the professional. Your local tournament can mean as much to your junior as winning one of the Grand Slam tournaments does to a professional. Preparation through planning is the way to go. In this chapter I will discuss some planning methods that work for the pros, and that will also work for your developing junior.

Other than professionals, there are four basic types of tennis players who like to compete: the high school or tournament-level junior, the college athlete, the weekend warrior and the league player. Each of these groups has designated periods when most of the competition takes place. Every player in each of the categories has the ability to schedule his training in such a way that he will be playing his best when it counts. A junior player, for example, would want to be playing his best tennis during the competition season. The whole year's training should be geared toward having the player's game at peak level when the competition begins. A player doesn't want his body to be worn out when there are matches to be played. The pros do this by periodization — a training program that controls the duration, intensity, frequency and content of their workouts so they can peak at certain times of the year. Periodization works at all skill levels and ages.

Studies have shown that no individual can perform his absolute best 100% of the time. An individual can expect to peak only about four or five times a year. With periodization, an athlete can determine when he peaks, and by carefully planning training, he can reduce the risk of serious injuries. Periodization can be broken down into four stages: preparation stage, precompetition stage, competition stage and active rest.

Preparation Stage

During the preparation stage, your students should work on developing physical fitness and technical skills. Develop a program for enhancing their strength, quickness and agility. Start out on a low intensity level two to three times a week. Work on increasing their aerobic fitness for endurance, alternating days with strength training. Bicycling and running in moderation are the best ways to begin this part of training. Increase their intensity level gradually. The preparation stage is also the period to work on stroke production. Every player has a shot they depend on when playing a challenging opponent. Be sure your students practice their best shots, as well as the obvious strokes that need work. Every player needs a weapon. The preparation stage should last two to three months.

Precompetition Stage

During this stage of your students' training, begin to phase out their visits to the gym and cut their running by half. This gives their bodies time to recover so that they can focus on more tennis-specific drills. Hone in their tactical game by simulating match-play situations. The playing of points and reaction-type drills are recommended at this point in training. This stage of their training should last at least a month.

Competition Stage

This phase begins on the first day of the tennis season. If you've stuck to your plan, your players should be match tough. Now is the time for your students to believe in themselves and in your training. If they win a few matches, you both should be proud. If they lose a couple of matches, everyone can still be proud, even as they congratulate their opponent.

Active Rest

After the tennis season, it is important for your students to take a break for a while. Give their body time to recover from a long season of competition. If they keep working out, they'll just wear themselves out physically and mentally. But warn them not to turn into couch potatoes. Playing other sports can help athletes relax. I usually play golf during the off-season to help me relax. Tell your students to go out and have some fun. That's why it's called "active" rest.

PERCENTAGE TENNIS

What is percentage tennis? It means that in any situation, a player uses the shot that has the greatest chance of success. Playing the percentages is one of the fundamentals of successful tennis, especially at the junior levels. Another way to look at percentage tennis is to play in a way that will make the most of a player's strengths and minimize his weaknesses. All too often, I see juniors going for the wrong shot at the wrong time. But how do you know what the right shot for the right time is? That's difficult to determine. Every player's percentages are different due to different skill levels. My advice is to encourage your player to practice these strategies to help him work out the percentages for his own game.

Practice your serve – Many juniors don't take the time to practice their serves. Maybe it's a little boring to them, but nothing improves the chance of winning as much as simply getting the first serve in play. The best way for a player to put pressure on himself is to consistently miss the first serve. Many juniors go for the ace hoping to win easy points, only to wind up double faulting and losing the point. Players must focus on getting the first serve in, and they'll be in a much more commanding position for the rest of the point.

Always get the ball back – What does it take to win a tennis match? To win a tennis match, a player must simply hit the ball back over the net and between the lines one more time than the opponent. That about says it all, doesn't it? Every time a player gets the ball over the net and in play, he's still in the point. When the score is close, teach your junior to use the most reliable stroke.

Let your opponent make the errors – At the junior level the ball crosses the net fewer than 10 times on the majority of the points. That means a player probably hits the ball no more than five times in the course of a typical point. Train your junior to keep the ball in play, and the chances are that the opponent will make the first mistake.

During baseline rallies, hit ground strokes crosscourt – If ground strokes are hit crosscourt, the ball passes over the center portion of the net. The center portion is lower in height, thus increasing the percentages of keeping the ball in play. The court is also longer diagonally.

Hit approach shots down the line – The best percentage play when a player receives a short ball that he can move in on for an approach shot is to hit his shot down the line. By doing this, he'll be reducing the angle of his opponent's passing shot.

Angle your drop shots – Like an approach shot, the drop shot should be hit off a ball that lands short. When attempting a drop shot, the best percentage play is to angle the shot over the center of the net.

Favor your best return – Most junior players have a better forehand than backhand return of serve. Some may have better two-handed backhands. In either case, tell students to move over a couple of steps to gain a better position to hit their best shot. By moving over a little, they'll be inviting the server to hit to that side.

Hit your overheads crosscourt – When a player hits an overhead smash, he should be trying to win the point either directly or by drawing an error from the opponent. At the same time, players must be sure not to make an error by trying to be too precise. If students hit their smashes crosscourt, they'll have the most room and the greatest margin for error by their opponents.

Use a lob when deep behind the baseline – I call this shot the moon ball. Obviously a player is not in an offensive position when the opponent pins him back behind the baseline with a deep shot. If a player lobs his shot, he'll gain time to recover into a better court position.

JUNIORS AND SINGLES

Racquet technology combined with the improvement of the overall fitness of young players today has brought junior tennis to a new high. The game of tennis is not just about having fun anymore. In fact, at the top levels of junior tennis, it's like a business — and business is good. Whether your player is competing at a high level of competition or just playing for your local high school, the key to winning isn't just a slam-bang, power hitting game. You'll be able to teach your singles player better if you understand some of the basic ideas of singles strategy. I'm going to suggest some points that you can use in helping your student develop into a better singles player. Remember, though, that these are not the rules. If a particular strategy or idea isn't working, change it. By teaching your player to use his, you'll significantly increase his chances of winning.

Consistent strokes – Work to make strokes consistent. A better command of singles strategy won't win more matches unless a player has consistent strokes. Teach players to develop a reliable serve, make them practice smooth and controlled ground strokes, and sharpen their volleys.

First serves – The first serve should be the best serve, the one that will give an opponent the most trouble and may even win the point outright. If the first serve is missed, a player is in a vulnerable situation by having to hit a weaker second serve. Players should practice the serve for placement as well as pace. Using a little spin on serves will help in the consistency.

Playing it safe – When returning serves or hitting ground strokes, teach players not to try anything fancy. They should be satisfied with hitting the ball back over the net. Have students aim the ball at least three or four feet over the net to make it go deep in the opponent's backcourt.

Crosscourt to crosscourt – Crosscourt balls should be returned crosscourt. Students make fewer errors if they hit balls that come to them crosscourt. There are three reasons for that: they'll have more court in which to aim the ball; the ball will pass over the lowest part of the net; and they'll be returning the ball along the same path that it came. A shot is more difficult if the direction and path of the flight of the ball is changed.

Spin with spin – Many junior players seem to have great difficulty in coping with balls that are spinning sharply. I think that's because they make the mistake of trying to take the spin off the ball. Teach them to use the spin to their advantage. If a ball comes to a player with heavy topspin, he should slice the ball back. If a ball comes to him with heavy underspin, he can use topspin to return it. By keeping the ball spinning in the same direction, players will have more control over the ball.

Using the lob – Junior players often forget that the lob is just as useful as an offensive weapon as it is a defensive shot. Students should not only lob against the player with a weak overhead; they should also use the lob to force a net-rusher away from the net. If a player is taken out of position, he can use the lob to recover. If the opponent is crowding the net, teach players to try a quick lob with a little topspin as an alternative to a passing shot. This almost always catches opponents off guard.

Go for the Weakness

All players have weak points in their games. At the junior level, it's often the backhand or the overhead smash that is the culprit. It should take only a couple of games to find the chink in an opponent's armor. And when you do find it, teach players to attack those weaknesses. Be wary, though, because a player can occasionally make a weakness stronger by forcing the opponent to use that shot. A student may also take himself out of a rhythm trying to force his shot to his opponent's weak side.

Ungroove for the Opponent

Some juniors like to camp out on the baseline and play the entire match from there. When facing such an opponent, teach students to never let him get in a groove. Remind them that most tennis matches are won by the player who makes the fewest number of errors, not by hitting the most winners. The baseliner's strategy is to patiently wait until the other player makes the error. So students should mix up their shots to the steady baseliner. Have your junior move the ball around, keeping the opponent off balance in his anticipation: forehand to backhand, frontcourt to backcourt, and net to baseline. Keep the net rusher deep, and bring in the steady baseliner. Above all, teach students to keep the opponent guessing.

Blunting the Power Hitter

When up against a power player who hits everything hard, the worst thing a student can do is to try to outpower him. The power player can use that pace against your pupil. Instead, teach your student to take the pace off the ball and return the ball smoothly with direction and safety. That way the opponent will have to generate his own pace. The opponent may hit a winner every now and then, but chances are that he'll make more errors than winners.

Follow the Short Ball to the Net

When the opponent hits a shot that lands inside the service line, your players should hit an approach shot deep into the opponent's court and follow it to the net. As mentioned in the section on percentage tennis, approach shots should be hit down the line. By doing this, players pressure the opponent into attempting a more difficult passing shot crosscourt.

First Volleys

Whether following the first serve or an approach shot to the net, students should aim the first volley deep near the opponent's baseline. Keeping the opponent deep will give a player the advantage of gaining a better angle on the second volley. After the first volley is hit, a player should pause with a split-step just before the opponent hits the ball. The split-step will prepare the player to move in any direction and give him a better opportunity to cut off the opponent's attempt at a passing shot.

Should students serve and volley? Most juniors do not have a serve and volley strategy in their arsenal of shots. In knowing this, it's a good idea to help students develop a serve that will allow them to follow it into the net from time to time. This strategy may benefit their game as an element of surprise. Singles matches can often be won at the net when it is least expected.

DRILLS: TECHNIQUE AND TACTICS

Traditionally tennis has been taught with two elements of the game in mind: technique and tactics. The technical approach is taught by isolating each stroke in a closed environment while feeding the student balls in succession to perfect the technique of the stroke. The tactical approach is taught in an open environment and creates a situation where students face many variables such as shot-selection, movement and tactics. Both methods are equally important and teach technique and tactics independently. Players with technical weaknesses and players with a lack of understanding of the game are not capable of reaching their full potential. For players to reach a high level of performance, coaches need to integrate technical and tactical drills into their teaching. To help you teach this, each type of training drill is described below.

Fundamental Motor Skill Drills

Although there are specialized tools and equipment being used today, children traditionally learned fundamental skills such as throwing, catching, balancing, tracking, running and jumping by playing different sports and games. For example, soccer teaches balance in motion. Footwork and leaping abilities can be learned in basketball. Eye-hand coordination skills can be learned by playing baseball. Playing is fun, and it can help improve your tennis game.

Single-stroke Feeding Drills

These drills break tennis strokes into isolated segments and allow players to learn each stroke individually. These drills emphasize technique development and are typically taught to beginning players. Advanced players can benefit from single-stroke feeding drills when learning to execute specialized strokes such as drop shots, approach shots, spin serves and ground strokes.

Movement Drills

Also known as multi-ball drills, these drills focus on teaching players how to produce shots with optimal technique during movement and shot-producing situations. Tennis points are made up of shot sequences, and players are taught to make decisions based upon these offensive and defensive situations.

Rallying Drills

These drills should be introduced as soon as possible. The benefits of these drills are the consistency and controlled technique that are necessary in developing tactical requirements. These drills also help to develop good movement skills and the ability to change direction accurately.

Decision-Making Drills

Once players can maintain a steadily paced rally, introduce decision-making drills. Decisions do not have to be complicated and may simply require change of the spin, speed, direction, height or depth of the shot.

For example, during a baseline rally, one player hits a short ball, and the other attacks the net off the short ball and changes the trajectory and direction of the shot.

Match Play Situational Drills

Simulate match play when practicing and have a specific goal in mind. This is more effective than repetitive drilling and gives players more of a competitive attitude. For example, practice serve-and-volley and service-return situations.

GAME STYLES

What is a game style? Basically, it's the way the player uses the technical and tactical elements to play the game. As junior players develop solid fundamental skills, it becomes the coach's responsibility to help them develop game styles that are consistent with their abilities. As a young player improves his skills, a game style will begin to reveal itself. The player's talents provide a road map and a foundation for the coaches to build on. Finding the right game style to fit your junior's abilities is not an easy task. As an instructor, you should know his strengths and weaknesses. Whether it's preparation for high school tennis, college or the pro tour, this is a very important time in your junior's prospective tennis career. Traditionally there are four basic game styles: baseliners, counterpunchers, serve-and-volleyers and all-court players. I will try to help you make a decision on choosing your junior's game style by describing the four traditional styles in the following paragraphs.

Baseliners

Baseliners have the ability to dictate play from deep in the court. Possessing big ground strokes, they can hit winners from anywhere. Good aggressive baseliners also are extremely quick and agile. Most possess excellent control over their bodies, especially their center of gravity, enabling them to remain balanced during the execution of their powerful ground stroking. They are particularly effective when returning serve and usually use their own serve to draw weak returns from their opponents. Once the ball is in play, they use their weapons to dictate play from the baseline. Baseliners are usually very fit, possessing muscular strength, power, agility and quickness.

Counterpunchers

As the name implies, these players counter the aggressive play of their opponents. They tend to play farther back on the court than baseliners, usually hitting ground strokes with more spin and a higher net clearance. Consistency and ball control are their weapons. These players have the ability to hit accurate passing shots and well-controlled lobs and are masters of outlasting their opponents in the patience department. When attacked with an aggressive style of play, they are able to neutralize the effectiveness of their opponent's aggression with a skillful defensive game. Counterpunchers usually have the willingness to stay out on the court for as long as it takes to win a match. For this reason, they must be extremely fit. An attitude of "it ain't over till it's over" is what gives them the ability to run down every ball.

Serve-and-Volleyers

These players possess the ability to take control of the match with aggressive net play. They are equally skilled at two ways of closing in on the net. They have big, controlled serves and can easily follow to the net. They also can attack the net using pinpoint accuracy on their approach shots. They have outstanding volleying abilities with a good understanding of net coverage and positioning. They are usually better-than-average athletes, with good quickness and overall movement skills. This is a high-risk game style that demands an aggressive on-court personality in order to play effectively.

All-Court Players

All-court players have the ability to use styles of play as the situation dictates. They are extremely fit and have the ability to adapt to any situation. They don't possess any big weapons but can hit any shot in the book at will. They also have the unique skill of hitting the right shot at the right time. On-court decision-making as it relates to tactical adjustments and shot selection is their weapon.

Once you and your junior have decided what style of play best suits his skills and abilities, you can help that player cultivate the strategies, patterns, tactics and weapons necessary to implement that style on the tennis court. Start by building practice and training sessions that complement and promote improvement for that chosen style of play.

PERFORMANCE

The most common standard used in tennis to evaluate play is the score of the match. But when you think of play only in these terms, you aren't seeing the whole picture. We all want to win, but winning isn't the best way to measure how a player is improving. For instance, a player can play the best match of his or her short career and still lose. On the other hand, a player can play poorly and still win. When players are performing at their very best, their chances of winning are much better. Players can't control winning nearly as much as they can control their own performances. Therefore, focus on the performance of the player and not simply winning.

When evaluating a player's performance, you have to consider the skill of the opponent and other conditions; for example, the weather conditions, the type of court (clay or hard), whether the match is the first or second of the day. When you consider all of these factors, you can better understand how the score is a poor indicator of overall performance.

Our goal is not for our juniors play perfectly, but for them to reach their full potential. A player's full potential is his peak performance. When a player reaches his full potential in a match, he continues to improve as the match progresses. He seeks to play better with each and every point. We must set high expectations for them and encourage them to meet those expectations. To walk on the court and seek less is to have lower expectations for their performance and match play.

As instructors and coaches, we must spend more time teaching players how to play the game of tennis and not just how to hit the ball. If you are a new instructor, you may not possess the knowledge and skill to teach them more than ball striking. But if you are experienced enough, you should know that playing tennis involves physical performance, emotional control and mental performance.

Physical Performance

A junior's physical execution involves such things as stroke mechanics, footwork, movement and body rotation in the shot. The fitness and conditioning are also included and involve stamina, endurance, flexibility, coordination, agility, balance, quickness, speed and eye-hand skills. You can actually measure the physical performance of a player by the execution of his strokes and the level of conditioning the player shows during the match.

Emotional Control

Emotions affect how young players think, how hard they try, and how confident they are. Many juniors play poorly because of a lack of emotional stability in a match. Similarly, a young player's performance may be lacking because his emotions are not in check. Being overly emotional can have a negative impact on performance. Emotional play is measured by viewing body language, emotional reactions, the effort put forth, facial expressions and verbal responses.

Mental Performance

A young player's ability to win is directly related to his or her ability to think and make decisions on the court. Mental performance involves tactical decisions, shot selection, problem solving, effort, creativity and concentration.

JUNIORS ON CLAY

Young tennis players and their coaches often overlook one tool that can be a major component in training and playing – clay court tennis. Clay court tennis involves long points, big strokes and endless running and sliding. Every coach should integrate a clay court training routine into his young student's workout schedule. Clay court play teaches players to be patient and to play low-risk tennis. Players also learn to develop points, play defense, use spin, neutralize opponent's strengths, and develop footwork and balance naturally.

By allowing your juniors to participate in the clay court experience, you'll be helping them to develop a well-rounded game. In the United States, players grow up practicing and playing on hard courts, with very little exposure to clay. Their games are built primarily around taking the ball early, hitting the ball flat and trying to out-hit their opponent. Although there's nothing wrong with this style of play, it does not promote the good footwork and balance that clay demands. For example, if the hard-court style of hitting hard and flat isn't working and your player is losing the match, what can be done to change the outcome? Rather than trying to out-slug the player on the other side of the net, your player should change his or her style of play to a counterpunching style, with the hopes of outlasting the opponent and drawing errors. The consistent style of play learned on clay could possibly change the outcome of the match. By learning to play on all surfaces, players can make subtle changes in their playing styles, which will make them more effective on all courts. In short, learning to play on clay will make them better players.

One thing worthy of note is that hard courts can take a toll on joints, but clay courts can take a toll on muscles. Usually a coach or instructor will see a higher incidence of muscle strains and pulls on clay. Players often complain of heavy legs and fatigue when they begin playing on clay. Improving their strength, flexibility and anaerobic conditioning will help them play better clay court tennis. Clay courts make the ball bounce higher, so the chest and shoulders take more impact. A basic upper-body strength program that includes chest presses, lat pull-downs, and shoulder exercises that focus on rotator-cuff muscles will help your player get ready.

On hard courts a player can change direction easily and quickly. But on clay, he must learn how to slide into his shots. Sliding is part of the game, and your player has to learn to get the balance and rhythm down so that he can slide, make contact with the ball, and then accelerate in a new direction — all without losing his balance. Your player can practice this by doing shuffle-steps quickly across a court, with knees bent and center of gravity low. On a clay court, control and balance are more important than speed.

PLAYERS' RESPONSIBILITIES

As a teacher of players of all skill levels, I have found that the majority of elite junior players have many things in common. Their actions speak loudly, and we can all learn from these top-ranked players. The top junior players display a strong responsibility for everything that relates to their tennis. They regularly attend training sessions, take private lessons, participate in match play events, and know their win/loss records by heart. These players register themselves for tournaments, check in at the tournament desk, carry their bags before and after matches, and stay informed of upcoming tournaments and events.

As a coach, it is important that you urge your junior to take responsibility for his own game. Doing this will create an environment for faster improvement, and the knowledge and work ethic a player can establish by doing tasks himself are invaluable. A large number of players lack the self-discipline and control needed to get a firm grip on their level of performance. Doing the little things I've mentioned can help your junior get to the next level. The competence and confidence factors are directly related to the responsibility factor.

Many times parents are a hindrance to a player developing responsibility. Allowing junior players at the tournament level to do small tasks, such as check themselves in at tournaments, check on upcoming competitions, carry their own bags, and set up their own matches and practice sessions, is very important. If parents are too involved, players can adopt the idea that playing is a chore and not an exciting and fun sport. I encourage all junior players to take responsibility for their own games. I want them to obtain a notebook, write down their personal goals, chart their matches, set their playing schedule, track their improvement, start doing off-court conditioning, and properly identify their strengths and weaknesses with help from the coach, not the parents.

MEET THE PARENTS

Coaching and teaching juniors can be a very rewarding experience. However, one thing I did not expect when I began my teaching career was how much time and energy it would take to deal with the parents of players. As an instructor and coach, you will quickly learn there are basically two kinds of parents that have an impact on your teaching effectiveness — those that make your job harder, and those that make your job easier.

We've all witnessed the parent who sits too close to the court, constantly voices sarcastic or negative comments, and gestures at every error or missed opportunity. These parents often live through their child's tennis, base their worth as a parent on their child's success, and try to coach and interfere with their child's lessons by distracting the child to such a degree that the player becomes uptight and less motivated. Some parents place far too great an emphasis on winning and far too little on improving, competing and the simple joy of playing. Others may be unrealistic in their expectations of their child's ability and performance. Regardless of the reasons for these negative parental behaviors, it is likely that their children will not reach their full potential as tennis players.

The parents who make your job easier can actually help elevate their child's performance. Through my experience, I have learned that behind every great player is a devoted parent who sacrifices much to help their child achieve his tennis dreams. These parents provide considerable financial and organizational support. They also instill critical values in their child, such as hard work, respect for others and the discipline needed for competitive tennis. Effective tennis parents also keep the lines of communication open with the player's coach, and by doing so, they greatly enhance the coach's understanding of the player.

So given the two different roles that parents can play in the junior tennis experience, what does a coach do to effectively teach juniors? You must first realize that you can help the situation by creating better tennis parents. Begin by working hard to build trust. Be honest and open with the parents and listen to what they have to say. Help them to understand what their parental roles and responsibilities are and educate them on positive tennis-parenting behaviors. There are a number of things you can do to improve the parent-coach relationship. Some of these are described below:

Educate Parents

Some parents come to the courts completely devoid of a tennis frame of reference. Educate the parents on ways to help you help their child. Caution them about the common pitfalls parents can fall into when they become actively involved in their child's athletic activity. Take a proactive approach to working with parents. Starting parents of beginning players on the right foot and guiding them through the junior tennis experience is more effective than leaving them on their own.

Communicate With the Parents

As a coach, you are expected to bring extensive tennis knowledge into the picture. Parents can also bring extensive knowledge into the picture where their child is concerned. They can provide you with a wealth of information to help you be more successful. They can advise you on the mental capabilities and emotional limitations of the child. These factors can have a huge impact on your teaching effectiveness. But these aren't the only factors to consider. You must also realize that the parents are your employers. And like any business, to be successful, one must listen to and meet the customer's needs. It is imperative that you develop excellent lines of communication and work to keep those lines open.

Prepare for the Parent Problem

Despite all of your efforts, from time to time you may have a problem parent to deal with. You want to be prepared to deal with them effectively before the problem occurs. Take some time to determine what parental actions you will not tolerate and how you might deal with potential problems. If you have these things figured out ahead of time, you will be more effective when problems begin to reveal themselves.

Part 4
Conditioning, Fitness and Strength Training

The full tennis-teaching package is only complete if the instructor has a wide base of knowledge, including a background in fitness, conditioning and strength training. One of the misconceptions in the tennis world is that a player gets in shape by just playing or taking part in competitions. If a stationary level of performance and a few limited skills is your goal, then engaging only in your sport will keep you there.

If, however, you want the utmost efficiency, consistent improvement and balanced abilities, you must participate in year-round conditioning programs. The bottom line in sports conditioning and fitness training is stress. Not mental stress, but adaptive body stress. Athletes must put their bodies under a certain amount of stress to increase their physical capabilities.

THE COMPONENTS OF FITNESS

Strength – the extent to which muscles can exert force by contracting against resistance.

Power – the ability to exert maximum muscular contraction instantly in an explosive burst of movements.

Agility – the ability to perform a series of explosive power movements in rapid succession in opposing directions.

Balance – the ability to control the body's position, either stationary or moving.

Flexibility – the ability to achieve an extended range of motion without being impeded by excess tissue such as fat or muscle.

Local muscle endurance – a single muscle's ability to perform sustained work.

Cardiovascular endurance – the heart's ability to deliver blood to working muscles and the muscles' ability to use it.

Strength endurance – a muscle's ability to perform a maximum contracture time after time.

Coordination – the ability to integrate the above-listed components so that effective movements are achieved.

Tell your students that when they are watching professional players at a tournament or on television to notice that the players seem to be tireless and have unbelievable strength and endurance. This superhuman ability is not something they're born with. They have to work at it. Even after the longest of points, they're ready to keep going. Even though most average tennis players will never possess the physical abilities of a seasoned professional, they still want to play to the best of their abilities. Just playing tennis does improve overall fitness, but if your students want to win more matches they'll need a proper exercise program.

Believe it or not, they don't have to spend a lot of money at the gym to start improving their fitness. All players really need is a body and the desire to improve. Many recreational players believe that all a player needs to be physically fit for tennis is to hit a lot of balls and run down every shot. This can't be further from the truth. At any level of competition, tennis courts can be damaging to the body. The more competitive a player is, the more he calls upon the body to tolerate the constant acceleration and deceleration on a hard surface. Aggressive movement on any tennis court takes training.

TYPES OF TRAINING

Interval training is known as anaerobic conditioning. The lungs and heart can't get oxygen to the muscles quickly enough to keep them from getting tired. To help the muscles create the energy without it, athletes need to train. I recommend having students run sprints in intervals with periodic bursts of speed, followed by brief rest periods. Interval workouts are necessary for tennis players because they turn on anaerobic power for a few seconds and then cut back to gear up for the next point.

Interval sprints

Cross-training, or impact training, is basically distance running on various terrains. Impact training is a necessity in developing a high-impact game. All students need to do is put on some running clothes and start moving. They can go to the track at the local high school or just put on some sneakers and cut the block. Some players believe that it's bad for the body, but that's not true. They get injured running because they don't run enough. I recommend players run at least three or four times a week. They can start with a quarter of a mile and work their way up. Running more than two or three miles at a time could be considered overkill.

Cross-training can also include playing different sports that complement tennis by using some of the same muscles. I played a lot of basketball. The mental and physical demands of basketball often mirror those of tennis. Lateral movement, sprinting and changing direction are all elements of both basketball and tennis. Soccer would be another sport that complements tennis. Soccer is "balance in motion" while getting anaerobic and aerobic workouts.

Directional drills, or footwork drills, are designed to improve a player's movement in any direction on the court. When playing, players are moving all over the place — corner to corner, net to baseline and diagonally. In order to reach more balls on the court, multi-directional drills are an essential.

To improve footwork at the net, I recommend directional volley drills.

To improve movement at the baseline, have players perform crossover and shuffle drills.

Base conditioning, or steady-paced training, should be the foundation of the rest of your students' conditioning and training. Some forms of steady-paced training are jogging, bicycling and elliptical machines. Working on base conditioning twice a week, 30-45 minutes a day is more than enough to build on. While anaerobic intervals help athletes play longer, developing an aerobic base is important in helping get through the final set of a match. Running out of gas is a good way to lose to a less-skillful player.

BREAKDOWN FOR INTERVAL TRAINING

The intensity level of your students' training depends on their age and skill level. Younger players and those who primarily play singles should do a more intense series of intervals and high-impact activities. Older players and those who primarily play doubles should gas up for lower intensity levels.

Players in their 20s and 30s

- Warm up for five minutes at moderate intensity.

- Sprint for 60 seconds at high intensity.

- Cool down for 60 seconds.

- Repeat the sprint-recovery series five more times, for a total of six sprints.

Players over 40

- Warm up for five minutes at moderate intensity.

- Sprint for 60 seconds at high intensity.

- Cool down for 60 seconds.

- Repeat the sprint-recovery series four more times, for a total of five sprints.

BREAKDOWN FOR CROSS-TRAINING

For distance running, I recommend a moderate pace for most age groups. The terrain specifications are up to the individual. For most players under 40 years of age, 30 minutes is more than enough at almost any skill level. For runners over 40, I recommend no more than 15 minutes on relatively flat running surfaces. Running on a track or solid ground is preferred over concrete or highways.

Players in their 20s and 30s

- Warm up for five minutes.

- Steady-pace jogging for 15-25 minutes.

- Optional: Take a 60-second breather every five minutes.

- Cool down for five minutes.

Players over 40

- Warm up for five minutes.

- Steady-paced jogging for 10 minutes.

- Optional: Take a 60-second breather after five minutes.

- Cool down for five minutes.

PLYOMETRICS

Plyometrics is simply a fancy word for "jump training." Professional players use it to improve explosiveness. This kind of training can help your students reach more balls on the court. Exploding into the general area of the ball gives an athlete more time to execute the shot. That's the difference in today's power game. The athletes are much stronger than they used to be. Sure, racquet technology has a little to do with it, but mostly it's about physical conditioning. The tennis players today even look like soccer players. Tennis is now a game of physical power. Even though there is an entire science dedicated to the study of plyometrics, to keep from overtraining the body, your students should start out with only a few moderate jumping exercises. To increase explosiveness, have them integrate single-leg jumps, exploding leg jumps, plyo push-ups and squat jumps into their routine. On the next few pages, I will provide a description of the exercises, complete with photo illustrations.

Single-Leg Jumps

The athlete begins by standing on one leg. He then lowers himself into a squat position while trying to remain balanced, then thrusts upward. Arms are used to help generate the power to extend upward. The chin must be kept up as the player tries to land softly on the same leg. Have students repeat this movement 5-10 times in succession and then switch sides. Have your players start with a series of two and move up gradually.

Exploding Leg Jumps

A player begins by placing the left foot on a bench 12-24 inches high, depending on his height. He must raise his arms to help generate power and then thrust upward to stand on the bench, with the left leg fully extended. Again, it is important for the athlete to keep his chin up and land softly on the court with the right foot. This movement is to be repeated 5-10 times in succession before switching sides. Have your players start with a series of two and move up gradually.

Plyo Push-Ups

Have your students stretch out facedown on the floor, with the hands placed slightly wider than their shoulders and legs extended, toes on the floor. Keeping the body in a straight line, they will lower themselves until their forearms are at a 90-degree angle to the torso. From this position, they must push themselves up quickly and powerfully until their hands leave the floor. Have them repeat this movement 12-15 times.

Squat Jumps

Have players start by standing with their feet shoulder-width apart. With the chest lifted and the chin up, they will squat down and then jump to get fully extended, using the arms for more height. Coach the players to land softly, working through their feet: toe, ball, heel. Have them repeat this movement 5-10 times in succession. They should start with a series of two and move up gradually.

CARDIO TENNIS

What is Cardio Tennis? It is an aerobic-style class on a tennis court. It is taught at hundreds of clubs around the world and the United States by certified tennis-teaching professionals. It includes a short dynamic warm-up, a cardio workout and a cool-down phase. Most of the Cardio Tennis program focuses on the workout phase, which should last up to 50 minutes. Much of this phase includes fast-paced drills during which the tennis professional feeds balls to players based on their ability and fitness level. The pros find ways to keep players moving and challenged while having fun.

The key is to keep participants moving at all times. There is no wait time. Drill-based exercises are fast and pros don't stop to correct strokes or technique. For play-based exercises, participants rotate in and out quickly as they play out singles, doubles, or even triples points. Between points, players may run through sideline drills that often use jump ropes, cones and other equipment.

Cardio Tennis pushes your players' fitness to a new level with a high-energy workout. The class features drills that get the heart pumping. This workout benefits players by burning more calories than singles or doubles play, and by providing short cycles of high-intensity workout and periods of rest. "Get Fit, Have Fun" is the tagline for the organization. You can find out more about Cardio Tennis by getting in touch with your local Professional Tennis Registry (PTR) professional, your local United States Professional Tennis Association (USPTA) professional, or by logging onto www.CardioTennis.com.

STRENGTH TRAINING AND CONDITIONING

An important and sometimes overlooked aspect of training for competitive levels is strength training and conditioning. I feel that all instructors and coaches should have a solid base of knowledge in this area if they are serious about becoming professional tennis instructors. That is the reason I've included facts about strength training and conditioning in this guide.

Strength training is a critical component to the success of an athlete. By becoming stronger and increasing muscular endurance, an athlete is able to perform more efficiently and is better able to avoid injury. Furthermore, there are a number of other physiological adaptations to strength training. The strength of tendons and ligaments is increased. Bone density increases, making the bones stronger and more resistant to fractures. And the maximum heart rate is improved, increasing metabolism.

Designing a strength-training program is often an annoying process for the nonprofessional. Hopefully the following information will provide some insight into the process and encourage you to implement resistance training in your students' weekly fitness sessions.

There are six essential program variables to consider when designing a weight-training program. These include a needs analysis, exercise selection, training frequency, exercise order, training load and repetitions, and rest periods.

Needs Analysis

Needs analysis refers to a two-stage process that considers the sport the athlete is training for and the training history of the athlete. The unique characteristics of the sport must be considered in planning a regimen to make the training as specific as possible. Specific muscular movement patterns, cardiovascular endurance needs and flexibility requirements are all important considerations. The current level of fitness, the training experience and the medical history of the athlete are also integral when planning a regimen. For example, if an athlete has a history of ankle sprains and at present has an unstable ankle joint, balance and intrinsic foot and ankle strength will be included in his program.

Exercise Selection

Exercise selection deals with choosing exercises that reflect the needs of the athlete's sport, with consideration paid to the athlete's training history. For example, let's look at two different types of weight-resistant exercises: core exercises and assistance exercises. Core exercises recruit larger muscles that are primary movers at one or more joints. These core exercises stabilize the proximal segments of the body, allowing for fine motor patterns at the extremities. Assistance exercises recruit smaller muscles, such as the biceps or calves, that are considered less important in athletic performance. In addition, exercise selection should be as sport-specific as possible. Specificity training provides the best likelihood of transfer to performance. For example, forward and lateral lunges would be a sport-specific exercise for a tennis player or a pitcher in baseball.

Training Frequency

Training frequency refers to the number of training sessions in a given period of time. Again, the goals of training and the experience of the athlete must be taken into consideration when planning training frequency. Traditionally, three workouts per week are recommended for many athletes, as the intervening days allow for sufficient muscular recovery between sessions. Athletes with less experience with weight training should begin with fewer sessions per week.

Exercise Order

Exercise order involves the sequencing of exercises during a training session. Decisions should be based on how the athlete responds to specific exercises and how the exercises performed first will affect exercises performed later. Typically, exercises that require the most refined technique and recruit the larger prime movers are performed first, followed by assistance exercises. For example, a single-leg balance squat should be performed before a one-leg calf extension. Another method that allows for adequate recovery involves alternating between upper- and lower-body exercises.

Training Load And Repetitions

The training load is the amount of weight lifted, and repetitions are the number of times the weight is lifted. Typically, there is an inverse relationship between load and repetition. This means if the amount of weight lifted is high, the number of repetitions is low and vice versa. The load lifted usually depends on the goals of the training program. For example, a resistance program geared for gains in muscular strength requires lifting heavier loads and fewer repetitions. Conversely, a program geared toward muscular endurance or toning requires lower loads and higher repetitions.

Rest Intervals

Rest intervals are the periods of time between exercises. Rest intervals are based on exercise experience and the goals of training. An athlete with limited weight training experience will need more time for muscle recovery between sets. The other variable when considering rest intervals is the training goal. When training for strength or power gains, the rest interval is between two to five minutes. If muscular endurance is the goal, rest intervals should be between 30-90 seconds.

Strength Training

Almost every tennis player, at one time or another, has been in position to hit a ball, but then didn't have what it took to get the ball back. Sometimes it takes more than technique and timing to up some mustard on shots. When you think about getting your players ready for the competitive season, they just can't step out and play without muscle to support their body or their shots. A trip to the gym a couple days a week can drastically increase their strength on the court and improve their ability to pull off some great shots.

Strength training is basically resistance training that uses the principle of progressive overload to force the body to adapt in order to be able to produce and resist greater forces. Strength training is not power lifting, nor is it bodybuilding. In fact, athletes don't have to use weights at all. Their body weight can provide enough resistance to train for tennis. In today's power game of tennis, strength training and conditioning are becoming necessities. Players are moving faster and hitting the ball harder with unbelievable angles from all over the court. Strength training in tennis can help to prevent injury and enhance on-court performance.

When your players get to the gym, tell them to focus on exercises that involve pushing and pulling small amounts of weight in the beginning. Pushing and pulling helps balance the body. Two or three days a week, they should strength train doing primarily multi-joint exercises, including lightweight leg and chest presses, lat pull-downs, lunges, squats and push-ups. When I played competitive tennis, my strength trainer told me to "focus on the muscles you can see in the mirror."

They should also focus on the core muscles, which provide stability in all movement and play a significant role in protecting and supporting the spine. Sit-ups and the use of gym equipment that concentrates on twisting and turning are helpful in strengthening core muscles. Every athlete's success stems from the core, the area of the body consisting of the abs and lower-back muscles. If the core is stable and strong, all other movements become more efficient and effective.

Make sure your students don't ignore the smaller muscles. The wrists and forearms are used for direction and disguise in executing shots. It's also important for your students to do some light stretching when they complete their workout to keep the muscles flexible. Have them start by doing two to three sets of 10-15 repetitions, using no more than 50-100 pounds of weight on the arms and legs and no more than 5-10 pounds on the wrists and forearms. Two or three times a week is a good start, and your players can increase the frequency and weight after a couple of weeks.

Remind your students that it's possible to overdo it. If they're not familiar with strength training or haven't done it in a while, they should start into it slowly. Gradually have them make it a regular part of their training routine. It only takes about 30 minutes per training session to feel and see the results. Staying longer in the gym doesn't necessarily mean they'll get faster results. The only thing they'll produce is longer recovery periods or injuries. If your students can afford it, suggest that they hire a trainer to get started safely.

Principles Of Conditioning

1. Tell your students to match exercises to their weaknesses and needs. For example, any posture defects such as protruding shoulder blades, round back, scoliosis, flat feet, knock-knees or bowlegs may become worse with strength and endurance training. Well-designed strength training may help, but it must be designed to specifically address these problems. Players should get their physician's approval for strength and endurance training.

2. Players should develop aerobic fitness before attempting intensive strength training. For example, weightlifters with insufficient aerobic fitness recover more slowly than the well-prepared ones. The level of lactate after a workout is higher and stays high longer for those with insufficient aerobic fitness.

3. Players must build a strong muscular and skeletal structure before attempting sport-specific strength and endurance exercises.

4. Tell your students to work on developing flexibility before increasing resistance. Strength exercises initially use light loads that permit a full range of motion.

5. Students should develop the core of their bodies before the extremities because their limbs can generate only as much force as the trunk can transfer. No matter how strong the legs are, the forces generated by the legs will eventually damage the lower back if it is not strong enough to stay in proper alignment.

6. The muscles that stabilize the joints (elbows, wrists, shoulders and knees) should be developed because the amount of force joints can produce is limited by what the muscles can withstand. When a player moves quickly or produces a stroke, and the muscles of his wrist or elbow, or shoulder are too weak to stabilize these joints, he loses force because of poor alignment. With repetitions a player will gradually damage those joints. Stabilizing the joints will give a solid base for their action.

7. Make sure your students balance the exercises around any joint so the tension of all the muscles that control the joint is in balance. When the strength of the muscles around a joint is balanced, no one muscle group pulls the joint out of its natural alignment.

8. Players should start with general conditioning exercises and progress to sport-specific exercises. General strength exercises lay a foundation for sport-specific ones by strengthening all major groups of muscles around each joint in a balanced way. General strength exercises prevent injuries.

   All strength exercises cause both structural changes (increased number of mitochondria, capillaries, amount of muscle glycogen, size of muscle fibers, structure of connective tissue, and density of bones associated with the exercised muscles) and functional changes in the neuromuscular system. The changes caused by strength exercises in the neuromuscular system are specific for each type of exercise, which is why your players need to progress from general to sport-specific exercises. Only beginners can experience sport-specific improvement for general exercises.

9. Players should use natural movements for both the general and sport-specific strength exercises. Do not have them isolate muscle groups with artificial, bodybuilding-type exercises. There is no isolation in any natural movement, be it lifting, jumping, pushing or pulling, and there is no isolation in any of their techniques. Isolation is a concept of bodybuilding and is appearance oriented. It has little or no application in strength training for action. If possible, your players should do general strength exercises in the same movement pattern as their technique.

10. Beginners should use the smallest resistance that

still increases strength. With beginners (either young athletes or adults who never did serious strength training), the strength increase does not depend on the amount of resistance as long as that resistance is more than the minimum required for the training effect. For beginners, that minimum may start at more than 20% of their personal best. The strength of a muscle's contraction depends on nervous activation, energy supplies in the muscle, the cross-section of the muscle, and its ability to recover after work. All these factors are interdependent, but they do not develop at the same pace. This is another reason not to use maximum loads at any given stage of training.

11. The pace of exercises determines the result. In strength exercises a slow pace increases the resistance by eliminating the momentum of the weight and thus develops hypertrophy. A fast pace reduces the resistance (taking advantage of momentum) but improves mobilization and synchronization of motor units and so develops the type of functional strength needed for tennis.

12. Increase the load (resistance, distance, pace) gradually so your student's whole body has time to adapt to it. The pace at which training loads are increased must be correlated to the pace at which the body adapts. The body adapts itself to each new load with a certain delay. The delay depends on the volume and intensity of the load. This ability depends on age and other factors. An abrupt increase of the load may surpass the body's ability to adapt and result in over-training or injuries.

13. Tell your students to get enough rest between workouts so their bodies can recover and be able to work harder and better in the next workout. Recovery time after exercises depends on the mass of exercised muscles. Small muscle groups such as those of the forearm or the calf can recover in less than 12 hours. After exercises such as squats, which fatigue a large mass of muscles, the recovery may take more than 48 hours. Also, your body's various systems (nervous, muscular, cardiovascular) recover at different rates after the same exercise. This lets your students work out every day or even several times per day, as long as each consecutive workout stresses the system that has sufficiently recovered.

14. Help plan your students' training so they can peak when needed. They do not want to be in top shape long before or long after the tennis season. They want to be their best when it matters most.

STRENGTH TRAINING AND JUNIORS

There are many questions surrounding strength training, especially where children are concerned. The risk of injury is a primary concern of any parent or coach who has a child entering strength-training programs. Many parents and coaches are hesitant to begin strength training with juniors for fear of damaging the bones and possibly stunting growth.

Any activity or exercise comes with some level of injury risk, but youth strength training can be safe and effective if a competent coach who is skilled in program design supervises every training session. Proper technique must be taught and is required in every repetition of every exercise. I strongly recommend that children do not train without professional supervision. If you are experienced enough in the gym to proceed with a junior program, ask yourself two questions first: "Is the child physically and emotionally mature enough to engage in a strength-training program?" and "If you are using machines or equipment, is it sized appropriately for a child?" Players need to show the maturity, both physically and mentally, to advance into a weight-training program. Most equipment is sized to meet the needs of adults, not children. Make sure there is equipment that can adjust to the size of a child. If not, wait until the child grows into the equipment.

Strength training does work for juniors. If the program is properly supervised, the child's motor control and strength will increase by teaching the muscles how to work together. That will lead to improvement in strength, self-image and self-confidence without increased muscle mass.

BODY-WEIGHT EXERCISES

Be sure your students understand that they don't have to spend a lot of money on gym memberships or fancy workout machines. One of the best pieces of exercise equipment is staring back at them in the mirror. It's not only free, it's something that each individual already has. Without any added weight, the body can provide all the resistance needed for a functional strength-training workout. It's also safer, easier to use and more practical for developing tennis-specific strength for the courts. Some of the primary benefits of body-weight exercises are:

1. Body-weight exercises force athletes to be aware of their own body.

2. They help maintain control over the entire body.

3. The core is engaged in each movement.

4. The exercises promote good posture.

When an athlete uses free weights, he works muscles in isolation. This can lead to an imbalance in training. Working muscles in isolation can increase their size and strength, but it can't train them to work optimally in real-life situations. A person can be a strong weight lifter, but if he wants to be a tennis player, he has to have functional strength he can apply to on-court situations. Sitting on a machine in the gym is not the way an athlete moves on the court.

Body-weight exercises can be described as systematic bodily exercises without apparatus. Most people are familiar with basic calisthenic exercises such as sit-ups, crunches, squats and push-ups. There are a host of other exercises emphasizing agility, flexibility, endurance and cardio exertion that will help develop a higher functional strength and body awareness.

THE IMPORTANCE OF STRETCHING

At any athletic event, you'll most likely see players stretching various parts of their bodies in preparation for competition. But did you know that certain types of stretching before play actually can reduce the amount of power your muscles generate and negatively affect your performance? The stretching that most average players are familiar with, static stretching, is accomplished by putting the muscles under light tension held 15-30 seconds. This type of stretching before play may not be helping performance. Static stretching is more appropriate and beneficial after play. Static stretching done after play or training is recommended for increasing and maintaining overall flexibility.

Dynamic stretching is what tennis players should do before playing. It's essentially stretching with movement, and it represents a new way of preparing the body for athletic activity. Dynamic stretching warms up the body and involves movement that gradually increases reach, movement speed and reaction time. It consists of arm, leg and torso movements that take an athlete to the limits of his range of motion and help preserve the muscles' ability to generate power while preparing the body for activity. A player can design his own dynamic stretching routine. The routine should be 5-10 minutes long and consist of short warm-ups that emphasize forward and backward movement, lateral movement and multidirectional movement. It should also include routines that address a player's specific needs and target weak areas of movement. The idea is to gradually increase movements that will mirror what the body and muscles go through during match play. The routines you design do not have to be overly complicated or long. When the warm-up is finished, players should do some light hitting before hitting all-out. The benefits of a dynamic warm-up are as follows:

- A dynamic warm-up increases the body's temperature causing the muscles to contract more efficiently and generate greater force.

- It primes the cardiovascular system by preparing the heart and lungs to engage in vigorous activity.

- It actively elongates muscles, which will improve the joints' range of motion and the body's ability to handle the forces experienced during play.

- It helps to ingrain proper movement patterns, leading to better on-court performance.

- It wakes up the nervous system and prepares the brain to talk to the muscles, which allows the muscles to work more efficiently.

GENERAL MOBILITY EXERCISES

Improving general mobility has many benefits, including an increased range of motion, flexibility and injury prevention. Below is a list of general mobility exercises that should be in every athlete's training routine.

Shoulder Circles

The athlete must stand tall with good posture. He then raises his right shoulder toward his right ear and takes it backward, down and then up again with a smooth rhythm. After performing this shoulder-circling movement eight times, he repeats with the other shoulder. Make sure your students breathe easily throughout.

Arm Circles

The athlete starts by standing tall with good posture. He then lifts one arm forward and takes it backward in a continuous circling motion, keeping the spine long throughout. He should perform this arm-circling movement eight times before repeating the exercise with the other arm. Tell your students to avoid the tendency to arch the spin while carrying out the circling movement. They should breathe easily throughout.

Side Bends

Again, the athlete starts by standing tall with good posture. His feet should be slightly wider than shoulder-width apart, with the knees slightly bent and hands resting on the hips. He then lifts his trunk up and away from the hips and bends smoothly first to one side, then the other, avoiding the tendency to lean either forward or backward. He should repeat the whole sequence 16 times with a slow rhythm, breathing out as he bends to the side and in as he returns to the center.

Trunk Twists

The player starts by standing tall with good posture. His feet should be slightly wider than hip-width apart with the knees slightly bent. His hands are resting on his hips, with the spine long and hips facing forward. He should then turn smoothly and slowly around to one side, then the other. The sequence is repeated 16 times, with the player breathing easily throughout the movement.

Half-Squat

The player starts by standing tall, holding his hands out in front of him for balance. He then bends at the knees until the thighs are parallel with the floor. The back is kept long throughout the movement, and players should be looking straight ahead. The knees should always point in the same direction as the toes. At the player's lowest point, he should fully straighten his legs to return to the starting position. The exercise is to be repeated 16 times with a smooth, controlled rhythm. A player should breathe in as he descends and out as he rises.

Standing Calf Stretch

The exercise begins with the player standing tall and facing a wall, with one leg in front of the other near a wall. He then places his hands flat against the wall at shoulder height. Keeping his back leg straight and easing it farther away from the wall, he then presses his heel firmly into the floor. The hips remain facing the wall.

Tell your player he should feel the stretch in the calf of the rear leg. Have him repeat on the other side. He should breathe easily throughout the exercise. This should be performed three to six times and each stretch should be held for 5-10 seconds.

Lower Calf Stretch

The player is positioned in the same way as the standing calf stretch exercise. This time, however, he will bend the knee of the rear leg while still keeping the heel pressed firmly to the floor. The sensation of stretch should now be experienced in the lower calf. He then repeats the exercise on the other side, breathing easily throughout. Have him perform three to six stretches and hold each stretch for 5-10 seconds.

Seated Hamstring and Groin Stretch

The player starts by sitting tall with both legs fully outstretched. He then bends the right knee so that the right foot rests comfortably along the left inner thigh, and the right knee is turned out to the side as close as possible to the floor. Keeping the spine long and the shoulders down away from the ears, the player will bend forward from the hips and reach toward the flexed left foot. He should go as far forward as possible, then relax the spine to reach even farther forward, holding this stretch position. He should feel the stretch along the back of the outstretched leg and along the inside and rear of the flexed leg. Have the player repeat the exercise with the other leg, breathing easily throughout. He should perform three to six stretches and hold each stretch for 5-10 seconds.

Lying Quadriceps Stretch

The player starts by lying face down on the floor, with his forehead resting on his right hand. He then presses his hips firmly into the floor and brings his left foot up toward the buttocks, easing it closer to them with his right hand. He should feel the stretch along the front of the thigh. He should then repeat on the other side, breathing easily throughout the exercise. Each student should perform three to six stretches and hold each stretch for 5-10 seconds.

Hamstring Stretch

The player should lie flat on his back on the floor with his knees bent to approximately 90 degrees. Raising his left leg, he grasps it loosely behind the thigh with both hands. Then he should ease this leg as close to the chest as possible. Students should feel the stretch along the back of the flexed thigh. Next, he should repeat this exercise with the other leg. Make sure he breathes easily throughout. Have students perform three to six stretches and hold each stretch for 5-10 seconds.

Standing Hip and Thigh Stretch

The player starts by standing tall with good posture in front of a firm chair or stool. He then places the heel of one foot onto the chair back while easing his body toward this foot so that the chest and thigh come closer together. The hands rest loosely on the raised knee, and the spine and back leg are to remain straight. Shoulders must be kept down and away from the ears. The player will ease as far forward as possible and hold his position. He should feel the stretch along the front of the thigh of the extended leg and along the back of the thigh of the raised leg. Have students repeat the exercise on the other side, breathing easily throughout. They should perform three to six stretches and hold each stretch for 5-10 seconds.

Seated Groin Stretch

The exercise begins with the player sitting tall on the floor with good posture. He then eases his legs up toward the body and place the soles of the feet together, allowing the knees to ease out toward the floor. He should make sure that the back stays long and that the shoulders are down away from the ears. The hands should rest on the lower legs or ankles or by the student's sides for support. He should feel the stretch along the inside of the thighs and groin. It is important to breathe easily throughout the exercise. If your student wishes to stretch the hamstrings and hip extensors at the same time, he should ease forward by hinging at the hip, still keeping the spine long. He should perform three to six stretches and hold each stretch for 5-10 seconds.

Kneeling Hip Flexor Stretch

The exercise begins with the player kneeling on a mat or towel with one leg flexed in front. His weight should be evenly distributed so that his position is stable. He can also use his hands at either side of the body for extra support. His knee of the front leg is directly over the front foot. Keeping his spine long and shoulders down, he then pushes the hips forward from this position. He may find that he has to take the rear knee farther back before he can feel a stretch along the front of the thigh. He should then repeat on the other side, breathing easily throughout the exercise. Have your student perform three to six stretches and hold each stretch for 5-10 seconds.

Lying Hip Abductor Stretch

The player starts out lying on his back on the floor with both legs bent at the knee. He then crosses the left leg over the right knee, and uses the weight of the left leg to push the right leg toward the floor (the knee will be moving to the left). The back, shoulders and the foot of the lower leg must remain in contact with the floor throughout the movement. He should feel the stretch along the outside of the hip and thigh. Have the player repeat this exercise with the other leg. Make sure your students continue to breathe easily throughout the exercise. Each should perform three to six stretches and hold each stretch for 5-10 seconds.

Front of Trunk Stretch

The player begins lying face down on the floor, fully outstretched. He then brings both hands up by his shoulders for support and eases his chest off the floor in a "cobra" position, keeping his spine long and his hips firmly pressed into the ground. He should feel the stretch in the front of the trunk. Make sure students breathe easily throughout the exercise. Students should perform three to six stretches and hold each stretch for 5-10 seconds.

Seated Trunk Twist

The player begins by sitting tall with good posture, his legs stretched out in front of him with the spine long and the shoulders down away from the ears. He then places his right foot over his left leg by the left knee and rotates his trunk, using his left arm against his right knee to help ease him farther around. The right arm is on the floor for support. He should feel the stretch along the length of the spine as well as in the muscles around the right hip. Have students repeat on the opposite side, breathing easily throughout. Students should perform three to six stretches and hold each stretch for 5-10 seconds.

Upper Back Stretch

The player begins by standing or sitting tall with good posture. If standing, he should bend his knees slightly and tilt his pelvis under. He will then interlock his fingers and push his hands as far away from his chest as possible. Have him look down and allow the upper back to relax. Players will feel the stretch between their shoulder blades. They should breathe easily throughout. Have your student perform three to six stretches and hold each stretch for 5-10 seconds.

Chest Stretch

The player begins by standing with his knees bent slightly and his pelvis tilted under. He will then loosely clasp his hands on the small of his back. It is important to keep the spine long and the shoulders back and down away from the ears. Without arching the spine, the player must ease their elbows toward each other as far as possible, feeling the stretch in the front of the chest. Make sure your students are breathing easily throughout the exercise. They should perform three to six stretches and hold each stretch for 5-10 seconds.

Sideways Neck Stretch

Standing or sitting tall with good posture, the player must keep his spine long and his shoulders down and away from his ears. While keeping the neck long, he should tilt his head to the side and then repeat the movement to the other side. Have him perform three to six stretches and hold each stretch for 5-10 seconds.

Front of Shoulder Stretch

The player begins by sitting on a stool or standing tall with good posture. If standing, the player should bend his knees slightly and tilt his pelvis under. Then he places his hands behind him, interlocks his fingers and straightens his arms. Tell your student to try and lift the arms upward and backward as far as possible. Your student should keep the spine long throughout and make sure that his shoulders are back and down away from the ears. He should feel the stretch in the front of the chest. Make sure he breathes easily throughout the exercise. Have him perform three to six stretches and hold each stretch for 5-10 seconds.

Shoulder and Side Stretch

Sitting on a stool or standing tall with good posture, the player should bend his knees slightly and tilt his pelvis under. He then takes both hands above his head and places his right hand behind his head and as far down the spine as possible. He then uses his left hand to ease the right elbow closer toward his head, taking the elbow behind the head if possible. It is important that he keep the spine long and the shoulders down and away from the ears throughout the exercise. He should feel the stretch along the side of the trunk and shoulder. He must repeat the exercise on the opposite side, breathing easily throughout. Have students perform three to six stretches and hold each stretch for 5-10 seconds.

Part 5
Nutrition

Even at the junior level, competitive tennis requires massive amounts of energy. Most players put extra thought into what gear they will use on the court, but not everyone puts the same thought into what foods they put into their body. But proper nutrition will kick your performance level up a notch more quickly than spending a lot of money on gear. A tennis match involves literally hundreds of short bursts of energy over a 90-minute to two-hour time period. To maximize energy and performance, it's important to maintain a proper diet while consuming a lot of fluids.

CARBOHYDRATES

Carbohydrates are the primary fuel source for working muscles. They are stored in your body in tiny gas tanks in the form of glycogen. These little gas tanks are depleted during the course of a tennis match. Whether it's weightlifting, jogging or playing tennis, the best time to refuel is during the 30- to 45-minute window of opportunity after the workout. This is when the enzymes responsible for storing the energy are at their highest level. Think of it as a traffic jam that's just been cleared, leaving your energy highway open. Now is the time to hit the gas and give your body fuel in the form of carbohydrate-rich foods. Breads, rice, pasta, crackers, fruits and starchy vegetables such as potatoes and corn are appropriate forms of carbohydrate-based foods. Post-exercise snacks will start the glycogen storage process as well as provide broken-down muscles with fuel to rebuild and repair.

A common mistake players make is eating too close to match time. If an athlete is planning on a full meal before a match, he should eat at least two hours before playing. If he goes on the court sooner than that, he is setting the stage for nausea. Some players may be able to handle smaller amounts of food an hour before court time. Complex carbohydrates are the best choice for this meal. If he must have meat, he should eat chicken for protein or fish for the anti-inflammatory acids and to boost the immune system. Before a match, tennis players should consider foods with moderate fiber and lower fat content, such as a bagel or fresh fruit. To help with sodium losses during play, be sure to tell players not to be afraid to consume small amounts of salt in sports beverages or snacks such as pretzels or saltine crackers before they go onto the court. Although nutrition bars are also a source for energy and energy replacement, they are not the best choice. Here are some facts about energy bars:

- A typical nutrition bar weighs about 60 grams and contains 25 grams of carbohydrates (half starch and half sugar), 15 grams of fat (of which 3 grams are saturated). About one-quarter of the weight generally comes from water.

- Many nutrition bars claim to be low in salt and cholesterol, with a typical bar containing about 150 mg of sodium and generally fewer than 10 mg of cholesterol.

- Energy bars should not be used to replace healthful food choices regularly, because foods such as fruits and vegetables contain phytochemicals and nutrients that cannot be synthesized or added to bars.

EATING SMART

For many tennis players, tennis is a passionate trip through years of personal triumphs and failures. Whether it's to achieve athletic greatness or simply to socialize and escape a hectic lifestyle, tennis is a way to promote better health. Although playing tennis is not a cure-all from health problems, it definitely sets the stage for a better lifestyle. A tennis player's diet can be a solid foundation for a healthy lifestyle. Keep in mind that athletes should always consult a doctor or sports nutritionist when trying to design or change their diet. Below are some considerations for a smart eating plan:

Variety

By including a wide variety of foods from each food group, an athlete is helping himself consume essential vitamins and minerals. He should choose fruits and vegetables rich in color. Pick whole grain, wheat, bran and oat products. If he eats meat, select leaner choices such as chicken, turkey, pork and lean red meat. Athletes should pick enriched or fortified products.

Healthy Fats

An athlete should limit saturated fat intake by avoiding high fat animal products. He can choose fats that come from foods such as nuts, seeds, fish and olive oil. These types of fats promote heart health by controlling cholesterol.

Hunger

By concentrating on eating when hungry and stopping when full, an athlete will learn to eat what the body needs. Even if it's something an athlete really loves, he must learn to eat in moderation.

Food Supplements

As a coach, I promote food over supplements. However, there is a time and place for supplements. If your students have trouble eating a wide variety of foods, supplements might be worth considering.

HYDRATION

Tennis is a passion that many dedicated players refuse to give up even during the hottest days of summer. One of the biggest challenges a tennis player faces during the summer months is maintaining proper hydration. Dehydration can be a tennis player's most dangerous opponent, causing fatigue and a loss of strength and speed.

During exercise, an athlete body's core temperature rises. However, there are several mechanisms to help control this rise and prevent heat-related illnesses and injuries. Evaporation is the primary heat-dissipating mechanism, which is the reason sweating is so important. However, fluid loss as little as one to two percent of total body weight can compromise an athlete's tennis match by decreasing concentration, increasing fatigue, and decreasing reaction time. Further fluid loss of three percent or greater can compromise physiological function and dramatically increase the athlete's risk for heat-related illnesses or injuries.

First and foremost, it is important for tennis players, no matter what the skill level, to know the recommended amounts of fluid to drink. Secondly, they must learn how to apply these recommendations to their daily routines and competitions in order to optimize hydration and prevent potentially dangerous physiological complications. I recommend that my students chill at least two quarts of water the night before a match to drink during the match the next day. During competi-

Here are some tips for your students to help keep them cool:

1. Drink fluids before, during and after you play tennis or work out.

2. Don't wait until you feel thirsty; in the heat of a match, that will be too late to help you. Start drinking fluids during the warm-up.

3. Limit the intake of caffeine and milk products before you play.

4. Consider sports drinks rather than water alone. They can help boost your energy.

5. Test-drive sports drinks before using them during play to make sure the taste is agreeable and they don't upset your stomach.

Here are some interesting facts about sports drinks:

1. During workouts lasting longer than 90 minutes, an athlete's body may benefit from a sports drink.

2. Sports drinks have electrolytes and carbohydrates.

3. Carbohydrates in sports drinks provide extra energy. The most effective sports drinks contain 15-18 grams of carbohydrates in every eight ounces of fluid.

tions or training periods, consistent water consumption is essential in helping the body stay energized to compete. Drink somewhere between 8-10 ounces every two or three games. It's also a good idea to limit your intake of carbonated sodas, caffeinated beverages, coffee or anything with milk in it prior to or during a match or workout.

Water helps to cool and prevent dehydration, but it lacks energy boosters or sodium, so players may want to consider sports drinks that contain carbohydrates and electrolytes. Electrolytes are simply conductors of energy. These types of drinks can help players maintain power and speed for their shot-making and quickness around the court.

Immediately after the match, encourage players to start replenishing their body with fluids. Remember, the body's energy highways are open. Even after a student has stopped playing and the body has begun to cool down, he continues to lose water and sodium through perspiration. If a student has a tendency to sweat profusely, tell him to add a small amount of salt to his drinking water after the match to help recovery. It is also a good idea to take in fluids a few ounces at a time in order to receive the full benefit of hydration. Trying to replenish all at once can overfill an athlete's tank.

DAILY FUELING FOR PERFORMANCE

When your students walk on the court, do they complain of feeling tired or heavy? Do they take a long time to get warmed up? Are they resting well at night and feeling refreshed the next morning? If your students answer "no" to any of these questions, it could be a sign that they're not fueling their body with the right foods or the right amount of foods to help make energy and speed recovery after a long workout.

Sometimes tennis players think that leanness means quickness and therefore better performance. That couldn't be further from the truth. Being lean isn't always what makes a player's performance better. Staying strong and fueled with a proper balance of foods will help the body's performance more than any quick fix. Your players should follow a meal plan that helps them lose fat and increase lean mass. Daily fueling plans should include:

- A minimum of five servings of fruits and vegetables.

- A minimum of six servings of grain products—preferably whole grains to maximize fiber content.

- Two to three servings of lean meats.

- Three servings of lean dairy.

- Foods without sauces, butter or sugar to keep calorie content low.

- Minimal desserts, excess oils and alcohol.

Even with a well-rounded meal plan and training program, players may be tempted to dehydrate quickly to achieve a desired weight. This shortcut also impairs performance. To maximize performance, hydration must be maintained by replacing the sweat lost during an intense workout. Research shows that a sports drink consumed during training helps performance more than water. Selecting a beverage that contains carbohydrates, sodium and other electrolytes will enhance hydration.

ENERGY PLANS FOR MATCH PLAY

Your student may be an excellent player, but he won't get the most out of his skill if he doesn't eat the right thing at the right time. There are three distinct stages in every tennis player's match-day agenda: before a match, during a match and after a match. Nutritional needs are different for each stage. To give your players the best chance of success, you need to teach them to vary their eating habits to cater to their energy needs and match time.

Pre-Match Stage

On the day before a match your players need to build up their glycogen reserves. Chicken, pasta, beans and rice are recommended during this stage. They should not eat anything out of the ordinary, because nerves may cause their stomachs to be sensitive. Loading up on carbs for the first time or trying something new isn't smart. They should also be sure to hydrate more and boost their sodium, because they'll lose it when they sweat.

Match Day

Tennis requires intense bursts of energy. If a player can tolerate it, he'll need a 400-calorie meal including complex-carbohydrates and protein-based foods for energy. During play, the only drink an athlete needs is water. For a snack, a banana or a fig bar is a good choice, something that will be quickly available to use for energy and won't upset the stomach.

Post-Match

Athletes need protein to build muscle, so for the first few hours after the match, your students should load up on protein. Meats such as turkey, fish or chicken are recommended. Protein will help repair the muscles. The sooner the players can eat, the better. The body needs to recover as soon as possible to prepare for the next match. Lean red meats are also good, but be sure to stay away from hamburgers.

A SIMPLE WEIGHT-LOSS PLAN

Do your students want to improve court coverage? Tell them to lose some extra poundage and see what happens. Whether a pro or a twice-a-week enthusiast, every player needs a proper exercise program to play his or her best tennis. It will strengthen the muscles, build up stamina and, when combined with a few warm-up routines before matches, greatly reduce the chance of muscular injury. By keeping fit your students will improve their general health and more than likely reduce their weight by a few pounds. A few extra pounds can slow any athlete down on the court. Reaching optimal body weight can definitely improve a player's endurance and speed on the court. Assuming your students already have a decent exercise routine and don't over do it with diet too much, losing 10 extra pounds won't require anything drastic. If they trim 500 calories a day, they'll lose a pound a week. Tweaking the diet a little and adding a couple of 10-minute walks each day might be all it takes. Below are five minor changes that add up to roughly 500 calories.

1. *Whole grains for breakfast* – People who eat breakfast, especially whole-grain cereals, are less likely to be overweight than those who skip it or slam down ham and eggs and waffles and pancakes. I recommend a cereal that has at least five grams of fiber and is low in sugar.

2. *Fewer sports drinks* – Save sports drinks for heavy exercise. Unless a player is exercising for more than one hour, he should stick with water. Calories from sports beverages, juice and soda can add up quickly. Opt for eight ounces of water instead.

3. *10-minute walks* – Tell students to think consis-tency and not intensity. In addition to burning calories, two 10-minute walks added to a daily routine will aid in food digestion and will also reduce the amount of fat-producing insulin that's released into the body. Walks should follow meals.

4. *Meal size* – Athletes need to pay attention to por-tions. Your players might be eating the right foods, but too much of them. The reduction is simple. Put away the large plates and bowls. Using smaller plates and bowls may surprise your students when it comes to the benefits of weight loss. They may also want to measure their portions to be sure they are cutting back.

5. *Eating Speed* – Tell students to slow down when they sit down. Studies have shown that people who eat quickly consume more calories than people who were told to take their time. Tell stu-dents to eat slowly and eat less.

Part 6
Common Tennis Injuries

BACK PAIN

Every player knows that tennis can be particularly demanding upon the back. Lower back injuries may begin with back pain and spread into the hip and leg areas. If your students are experiencing a tingling or numbness anywhere below the waist, it could be related to a back injury. The constant running, bending, twisting, reaching, jumping and moving to reach the ball combined with the physical demands on the joints and discs are all reasons for the greater incidence of lower back pain associated with tennis.

So what can your students do to reduce the risk of a back injury? The muscles of the body are the only means athletes have to protect themselves from potential back injury. When a player contracts his muscles, he protects his joints as much as possible from the physical demands. Staying fit with weight training provides some protection. The area to concentrate on is the core or abdominal area. When the core is strong, an athlete is better able to stabilize the spine during physical activity. Briefly holding the breath during a physical demand can be a good thing. When an athlete holds his breath, he is contracting his abdominal muscles. This simple act helps to support the spine.

The gym offers a number of machines designed to strengthen the abdominal core muscles. One of the advantages of machines is that resistance can be added to enhance the intensity and results. To get the best results building strength, athletes need to focus on intense contractions and not a multitude of repetitions.

SHOULDER PAIN

Shoulder pain is known in the medical world as impingement syndrome or rotator cuff tendonitis. It is one of the most common overuse injuries occurring in tennis players. Symptoms include pain at the tip of the shoulder that occasionally radiates down the side of the arm. The pain is usually felt when serving or hitting overhead strokes. Often the symptoms progress to the point that lifting and reaching during everyday activities become painful. Eventually pain will develop when lying on the shoulder during sleep. Other signs include popping sensations in the shoulder when serving or hitting ground strokes, muscle spasm in the back of the shoulder and weakness in shoulder motion.

The tendons of the rotator cuff are located within a channel of bone between the shoulder blade and the upper arm bone. Overuse of the shoulder occurs when repeated overhead activity decreases the space between the two bones and impinges upon the tendons of the rotator cuff. Overuse is the most common cause of rotator cuff tendonitis. Some other causes include weak muscles, poor mechanics in stroke production, strenuous training and previous injuries. When the rotator cuff muscles are weak, more force is exerted on the tendons, causing inflammation and pain. Muscles around the shoulder blade are commonly skipped in weight training and can spasm and cause impingement problems. Prior trauma or surgery can put the shoulder at a disadvantage due to scar tissue and restriction of overhead motion and rotation of the shoulder joint. Shoulder injuries cannot only be caused by sports activities, but also by everyday activities that involve overhead

motion. Unfortunately, many of us in our busy lives delay a trip to the doctor, hoping the pain will subside and the injury will repair itself. This is not a good idea because a shoulder injury can develop slowly and progress significantly without a substantial increase in pain.

SHIN SPLINTS

Shin splints are a condition frequently experienced by runners and tennis players of all fitness levels. Shin splints are characterized by pain in the front and sides of the lower leg that develops and worsens during play or exercise. There may also be tenderness over the shin bone as well as pain when the toes or foot are bent forward.

To better understand the cause of shin splints, let's look at the anatomy of the lower leg. This area is a complex formation of interweaving and overcrossing muscles and tendons that support the two bones in the calf area. The pain associated with shin splints is a result of fatigue and trauma to the muscles and tendons where they are attached to the bones. In an effort to keep the foot, ankle and lower leg stable, the muscles may exert excessive force on the bones, which can result in the tendons being torn partially away from the bone. This stress is especially painful because the thin layer of soft tissue covering the bones is loaded with nerve fibers.

Overload is the primary cause of shin splints. Shin splints are commonly associated with sports that require a lot of running and with weight-bearing activities. However, it is not necessarily the added weight or force applied to the muscles and tendons that causes the problem. Instead, it is the sudden shock of repeated landings and changes of direction that is usually the culprit. The basic treatment for shin splints is to massage the area immediately with ice to reduce further inflammation and irritation. The ice serves as a quick-acting anti-inflammatory medication. At the first sign of pain in the shins, stop your student's activity. Trying to play or exercise through the soreness will only aggravate the condition and keep a player off the court longer.

ABOUT THE KNEES

A tennis player can expect to have a problem with at least one of his knees at some point in a tennis-playing career. The knee is the joint where two of the body's longest bones meet: the femur and the tibia, more commonly known as the thigh and shin bones. The knee is the hinge between these two levers. These two levers are held together by a system of tendons and ligaments that keep everything connected. The kneecap, or patella, acts as a cover protecting the soft tissues underneath from blows that may cause an injury.

When you think about what we ask the knees to do in tennis, the occasional injury is inevitable. The constant acceleration, deceleration and directional changes while supporting your body weight are what create situations for injuries to occur. Strengthening the muscles that surround the knee can help prevent injury. To make the joint stronger, we can reinforce it by strengthening the quadriceps and hamstrings, because they help guide the thigh and kneecap. Hip strength is also essential. Some muscles that start at the hips cross down to the knees to prevent them from buckling inward.

FOOT OR ANKLE INJURIES

Almost every athlete has experienced an injury to the foot or ankle at some point during exercise or play. It is probably the most common injury associated with any activity that involves a lot of stopping and starting. Here are some common foot or ankle injuries.

Achilles Tendon Injury

Playing tennis can lead to either a strain or tear of the Achilles tendon. Having good flexibility is the best preventative measure. Make sure your players always warm up. They need to stretch the Achilles area before playing hard and work on increasing flexibility in that area on off-court days.

Ankle Sprain

Ankle sprain occurs when ligaments are stretched or torn from their attachment on a bone. The majority of ankle sprains occur on the outside (lateral) of the ankle joint. Sprains can also occur on the inside (medial) of the ankle joint, but they are less common.

Heel Pain

Heel pain or heel spur syndrome is the inflammation of a ligament which runs from the heel to the ball of the foot. The bottom or inside of the foot may hurt when standing. If the foot flattens too much, the ligament may overstretch and become inflamed. If the foot doesn't flatten, the ligament may be pulled too tightly from trauma, which will eventually cause pain.

Stress Fracture

A stress fracture is a break in the bone that can be caused from repetitive action or a sudden acute movement that creates additional pressure on a bone in the foot.

TRAINING IMBALANCE

When I was younger, I had no idea that the human body was so fragile. How could tennis be so demanding? It's really not — until players begin to develop some skills. Ironic, isn't it? The better a player is, the harder the game is on the body. When you watch the pros, they appear to break the laws of physical movement. But have you noticed that some pros seem to disappear for a while, and then suddenly appear back on top? This is usually due to injury. Something happens to a wrist, ankle, back or shoulder. It could be a thousand different things.

Other than an accident on the court, such as tripping and falling, what causes injuries? There's a lot of mumbo jumbo to describe the pulling of a muscle or the tearing of a tendon, but what it all boils down to is an imbalance in training. During the weeks of training leading up to the competitive season, your students probably singled out specific muscles while ignoring others. If a player is using heavy weights, he should stay away from the bench presses, leg presses and bicep curls that can lead to an imbalance of muscle development. In short, isolating muscles can create good looks in the mirror, but when one group of muscles is getting overworked, it creates a recipe for disaster. An overworked muscle creates inefficiency, causing another muscle to pick up the slack. All tendons, ligaments and muscles have their limitations. Encourage your players to get with a trainer and ask for help setting up a plan to work all muscles equally.

In order to keep players on the court and off the sidelines, it's important to encourage them to take care of their bodies. When it comes to minor strains or a slight tweak, don't ignore it and tell them to challenge their body's limits. Doing this could push a player right off the courts and onto the sidelines. Areas such as the shoulders, elbows, hip, knees, wrists, lower back, ankles and feet are put to the test in the sort of total-body workout that tennis provides. Make it a point to tell students to take care of each and every part of the body. If a player thinks he may have an injury, don't fool around. If you have the expertise to treat the injury, treat it; if not, tell the player to see a doctor.

The type of injury that is most common is the overuse injury. Stresses on the upper body are caused by the repetitive nature of stroke production. The movements involved with ball striking require constant turning and twisting at the torso and aggressive manipulation of the arms and shoulders. With all of this going on, injuries are bound to happen, especially if your student's swing pattern and stroke production are not technically sound. Improper form can lead to injuries such as tennis elbow and shoulder pain. While conditioning is important regardless of level of fitness, injury can occur if a player does not use the proper biomechanical motion in play. If your student is struggling with a certain stroke, make sure to review proper technique.

Lower-body injuries in tennis are commonly caused by the stress of rapid starting, stopping and changing of direction. The hip and knee are prone to wear-and-tear injuries, resulting from quick and sudden movements. Rapid direction changes can make a tennis player more susceptible to ankle sprains, which often result from rolling over the ankle.

It's important to train and condition off the court in order to go the distance on the court. Being well prepared with more than adequate physical conditioning is the best way to avoid injuries. Perhaps the most important action you can take as a coach to prevent injury in a tennis student is to lead a good warm-up before allowing him to play. Warming up and stretching will increase the ability of the muscles to create more power and strength and to prevent potential injury.

TREATING INJURIES

Tennis can be a demanding, injury-producing sport. If your student incurs a tennis injury, he could risk more than losing a few games. He could be sidelined from tennis and other sports for months. Luckily, recreational players who don't hit as hard or as often as professional players have a lower risk of injury. But some tennis players, no matter what their skill level, are prone to injury. So whether your students head out to the local courts or for the pro tour, follow the prevention guidelines that I have shared with you, because their bodies will only take so much before they decide to shut down to prevent more serious injuries.

If your student is experiencing any pain, no matter how slight, don't hope that it will go away. If he feels that something isn't right, it probably isn't. Don't encourage students to pop a couple of pills and keep going. Get them off the court and tend to the pain before it becomes an injury.

Even if your students only hit the courts on week-ends, they probably know how painful and debilitating tennis elbow or a rolled ankle can be. Joint pain is a top complaint heard by doctors. We have over 140 different joints that allow us to perform thousands of motions on a tennis court and in everyday life. Whether in the ankles, knees, elbows, or shoulders, the joints' cartilage must be present, healthy and smooth for pain-free movement. More slippery than ice, cartilage makes it possible for the ends of the bones to slide smoothly and easily across each other.

Cartilage can be damaged by sudden trauma or a gradual build-up of many tiny injuries. If the cartilage surface becomes damaged, movement may become painful. As the joint degenerates, the joint lining becomes inflamed. It tries to solve the problem by producing more of the slick, watery substance that lubricates and nourishes the cartilage. But the fluid ends up flooding the joint space, causing swelling and perhaps more pain. All an athlete knows is that the elbow or knee really hurts, it's swollen, it's hard to bend, and he doesn't want to put any weight on it.

Tips for Students With Injuries

1. Ice the injured area immediately, or as soon as you can, to help reduce inflammation and swelling.

2. Compress the injured area with a restrictive device or wrap to prevent swelling.

3. Elevate the injured area to help prevent swelling.

4. Above all, rest your injured body part to give your damaged tissues time to heal.

Injuries are a part of life and a part of tennis. However, once an injury occurs, tell students to allow time to heal. During the acute recovery phase, teach them to follow the "R.I.C.E. Principles": Rest, Ice Compression and Elevation along with limited activity. If you're sure your student is injured, especially if he has a history of injuries or is just coming off an injury, start applying ice to the affected area, not heat. By applying ice, you will decrease blood flow to the area, which minimizes swelling. If your student is injured on the court or while training, make sure he is completely rehabilitated before he starts playing again. If you are not familiar with a specific player's injury, or if recovery time is prolonged, send your player to see a doctor.

Regaining range of motion and strength should begin as tolerated, or as directed by a doctor. Tell your students to use discomfort as a guide and avoid movements that cause pain. Once muscle strength and flexibility return, a player can slowly get back onto the court, working at about 50-70 percent of the maximum capacity for a few weeks. During the re-entry phase, functional drills for balance, agility and speed can be added as tolerated. Here are some drills to use with your players prior to allowing them to play tennis:

Sequence Drills

To begin the warm-up, have students progressively simulate the movements of the tennis stroke without hitting a ball. In the process, they will gradually increase body temperature, loosen muscles, and retain muscle memory. Have them perform a series of tennis-specific motions or strokes and simulate all the basic strokes in tennis for about one or two minutes each. Keep in mind, if your students tell you that any of these movements tweaks pain or discomfort, it should be stopped. Encourage students to listen to their own bodies.

Net Drills

Have students pick up their racquets and start hitting at the net with some easy volleys. They should stay on one side of the court to reduce the amount of movement. These should be one-step volleys between the waist and shoulders. Have them practice this drill for about 15 minutes.

Service Line Mini-Rally

Next, the students will move back to the service line and begin letting the ball bounce before hitting it. Again, they should stay on one side of the court as they rally forehands and backhands. Make sure students avoid overheads that require them to step farther back and reach up.

Baseline Rally

Students then make the progression back to the baseline, gradually picking up the pace on their shots. Again, they should use only half of the court or less. This will reduce the stress on their movement and help control their shots.

Serves

Depending on the type of serve your student hits, the serve can place a great deal of stress on his feet and shoulders. If a player's injury is in one of these areas, be extra cautious. Have him go through similar progressions from the service line to the baseline until hitting about 50 percent effort. If he has a full range of motion and is pain-free during and after the warm-up, he is definitely on the road to recovery.

INJURY PREVENTION THROUGH RELAXATION

Try to educate your students on the movement and limitations of their muscles. Relaxation during your students stretching routines and after match play is a must.

Teaching students to manage the signals from their body begins with relaxation. Quite simply, the muscles have been taught how to work. Relaxation is vital to successful muscle re-education. When a player doesn't use his muscles, they forget their job description. This often requires a learning process similar to that of many other skills. We have learned a skill such as hitting tennis balls in part due to our ability to relax and focus on the task at hand. Relaxation allows a player to become more aware of the body and the signals it sends.

There are three basic aspects of relaxation: breathing, releasing the muscles and unfocusing the concentration. The first step in relaxation is to learn how to breathe properly. Abdominal breathing is preferred over chest breathing. Improper chest breathing causes contraction of various muscles from neck to chest. Since relaxation of the muscle tissue is the desired result and not contraction, abdominal breathing is the method of choice. Teach students to allow the diaphragm to rise and fall as they inhale and exhale, resulting in total relaxation. Next, have them focus on letting their muscles go. Tell them not to hold themselves in a set position. Have them begin with the feet and relax every inch of the body from toe to head, one section at a time. As students work their way up, they should only focusing on breathing. If a player notices any imbalances in his relaxation, this could translate to an injury on the court. The third aspect is relaxing without focus or concentration. At this point, players should allow themselves to simply relax and settle. When a player concentrates, he can often create tension. This is one of the reasons that many tennis players suffer injuries at high-pressure moments.

The goal is to eventually have the breathing and relaxation become natural. This will carry over into your students' performances on and off the court.

SENIORS: FITNESS, INJURIES AND INJURY PREVENTION

As players age and engines begin to fail, staying fit becomes more difficult and general fitness becomes more important than training for a specific sport. For those who love tennis, age shouldn't be a deterrent from playing. A lot of information is available for older athletes regarding general fitness and sport-specific training.

Tennis is one way for older athletes to remain active while developing cardiovascular fitness, coordination, balance, speed and agility. In addition, it has been shown that impact exercise increases bone density and helps to keep the bones stronger. Furthermore, actively participating in individual or team sports has been shown to relieve stress and lower blood pressure. It is also now evident that regular, intensive muscle training can minimize or reverse age-related declines in muscle mass as well. However, tennis alone is not enough to maintain health and strength into our later years. Muscle retains its ability to resistance train well into our late decades. It is very important for older athletes to combine strength training with tennis and other cardiovascular exercises.

As players age, stretching becomes increasingly important before and after playing tennis. Any activity that involves quick starts, stops and impact puts the body at risk for sprains, strains and tissue tears. Proper stretching can help prevent these injuries. Tell older students to consult a sports medicine specialist for a tennis-specific routine that will protect against injury. If an injury does occur, early treatment by a specialist is recommended. Too often, tennis players play through the pain, fearing that games or tournaments will be missed. Sports medicine specialists can often offer treatment that allows continued practice and play with some level of moderation. However, in older players, recovery is often delayed, and injuries may require more intensive treatment.

Obviously, recovery in older players takes longer. With the introduction of anti-inflammatory medications and the help of a sports medicine specialist, older players can recover faster from injuries ranging from mild muscle strains to chronic repetitive overuse injuries.

In a nutshell, seniors who want to stay fit for tennis must commit to additional training, stretching, strengthening and injury prevention and treatment in order to compete or recreate.

PROTECTING YOURSELF FROM THE HEAT AND SUN

Tennis is primarily a sport that is played during the warm months. To continue to stay healthy and enjoy the tennis experience, there are some very simple steps your players can take to protect themselves from the sun's harmful rays and ward off the effects of playing in the heat. You need to make sure they take precautions to protect their skin from longterm exposure to the sun's ultraviolet radiation. UV rays can cause premature aging and has been associated with various types of skin cancer. If your players spend a lot of time in the sun, tell them to check the surface of their skin often to look for warning signs. The most important warning signs are new skin lesions that are changing in size, shape or color, or sores that won't heal. If your players see anything unusual, advise them to consult a physician. They should be particularly careful if they have been sunburnt in the past. The effects of sun exposure could show up much later.

Players should not only be concerned about the sun's harmful rays, but should also be aware of the effects of heat and humidity. Outdoor activity in high heat or humidity can take a toll on the body if a player is not properly prepared or used to the conditions. Summer conditions can increase the risk of heat exhaustion, heat cramps or heat stroke. Heat exhaustion is caused by excessive perspiration and dehydration. To avoid heat exhaustion, players must stay well-hydrated during play. Heat exhaustion is treated with rest, stretching and hydration.

The symptoms of heat exhaustion are:

- Profuse sweating

- Headache

- Dizziness

- Muscle cramps

- Decreased blood pressure

- Elevated heart rate

- General weakness

- Nausea or vomiting

- Visual disturbances

- Rapid, weak pulse

- Ashen gray skin

Heat stroke occurs when the body can no longer cool itself. Symptoms include hot and dry skin, irritability, confusion, significant decrease in blood pressure, rapid and strong pulse, feeling cold or clammy despite high outdoor temperatures, and reddened skin.

Some guidelines and tips for protecting your players (and yourself) from heat from the sun are:

- Schedule practice time for mornings and late afternoons.

- Whenever you can, take rest periods during play or practice in the shade or under shelter.

- If you experience heat cramps, stretch the affected muscle and rehydrate.

- Use sunblocking agents such as zinc oxide or titanium oxide to protect vulnerable areas, including the nose, lips and ears.

- Use sunscreens with high SPF numbers and reapply after sweating and towel-drying.

- Use sunscreens even on cloudy days. UV rays still reach the earth on cloudy days.

- Protect your face and head by wearing a hat.

- Examine your skin periodically, looking for any indications of skin cancer. Pay particular attention to the number, size, shape and color of pigmented areas.

About the Author

Steven White is a professional tennis instructor and former satellite tour player. He is certified with the Professional Tennis Registry, the world's largest international organization of tennis teachers and coaches. He is a life-long competitive player and enthusiast who has been teaching tennis since the early 1980s. Steven studied physical education with an emphasis in recreation while on an athletic scholarship at Francis Marion College in Florence, South Carolina, where he was the number one player on the men's tennis team. He later transferred to Coastal Carolina University near Myrtle Beach, South Carolina, where he continued his education while teaching at the Myrtle Beach Tennis Club. He completed additional special training at Van Der Meer Tennis University, Hilton Head Island, South Carolina, in stroke progressions and corrective techniques, lesson and practice organization, individual and group instruction, and drill organization. Steven is currently teaching at the Monroe Country Club and Hammond Park near Atlanta, Georgia.